Lucknow Ontario and Area in Photos, Saving Our History One Photo at a Time

Photography
by Barbara Raué
2012

Series Name:
Cruising Ontario

Book 24: Lucknow and Area

Cover photo: Lucknow Presbyterian Church

Series Name: Cruising Ontario

Book 1: London
Book 2: Dundas
Book 3: Hamilton
Book 4: Oakville
Book 5: Chesley
Book 6: Stoney Creek
Book 7: Waterdown
Book 8: Owen Sound
Book 9: Mount Forest
Book 10: Dundalk
Book 11: Burford and Area
Book 12: Waterford and Area
Book 13: Drumbo and Area
Book 14: Sheffield and Area
Book 15: Tavistock and Area
Book 16: Ancaster and Mount Hope
Book 17: Innerkip
Book 18: Brantford
Book 19: Burlington
Book 20: Guelph and Area
Book 21: Ayr
Book 22: Erin
Book 23: Goderich
Book 24: Lucknow and Area

Other Books by Barbara Raue

Coins of Gold

Arrows, Indians and Love

The Life and Times of Barbara
Volume 1: Inventions That Have Enhanced My Life
Volume 2: Entertainment That I Have Enjoyed
Volume 3: East Coast Trips
Volume 4: Olympics
Volume 5: Wonders of the World
Volume 6: Caribbean Cruises
Volume 7: Animals
Volume 8: Storms
Volume 9: Wars

Lucknow

Lucknow is a community located in Bruce County, Ontario, located at the junction of Bruce Roads 1 and 86. Lucknow has a strong Scottish heritage back to the late 1800s when the Lucknow Caledonian Games were held for twenty years. The village was named after Lucknow, India where, in 1857, a battle Indian Rebellion of 1857 took place between the native rebels and the British army. Eli Stauffer first settled here in 1856 where he constructed a dam and built a sawmill. In 1858, Ralph Miller built Balaclava House, a log tavern.

Dublin

Dublin was founded in 1849 when U. C. Lee opened a store, on Huron Road 8. A small stream enters the village at its northern limit. Salt was discovered at Seaforth, five miles to the west, and through the enterprising efforts of Joseph Kidd, salt was brought in conduit pipes to Dublin where salt blocks were built and provided employment to a large number of workmen. Mr. Kidd also built a sawmill, and a block of brick stores on Main Street.

Mitchell

Mitchell is located at the intersection of Highways 8 and 23, east of Seaforth and 20 kilometres west of Stratford. Mitchell was founded in 1836 by William Johnston, who laid out a town plot and local tavern, and John Hicks, one of the first settlers of the area, who erected a hotel near the Thames River, where the historic Hicks House Hotel building (now restored with stores and apartments) in downtown Mitchell stands. A sawmill was built in 1842, as well as new stores and businesses, contributing to the town's growth.

Walton

Walton is located at the intersection of Huron County Road 12 and Road 25, 45 kilometres east of Goderich. Situated at the junction of Morris, Grey and McKillop Townships on the Seaforth-to-Wroxeter trail, Walton is named for the English hometown of its founders John and Anna (Button) Hewitt. Hewitt was born in Walton in Buckinghamshire, England and married Anna Button there. They sailed for Upper Canada in 1843 and settled in this area. The American Civil War (1861-1865) generated a widespread economic boom. Soon there were two stores, a lodging house, a blacksmith shop, sawmill and gristmill. Rob Roy and Walton Hotels were built and postal service began in 1862 in one of the stores. The Walton Hotel was the most successful and it still functions as an inn and restaurant today. Through the years there were pump makers, butchers, barbers, jewellers, lawyers, blacksmiths, carriage makers, harness makers, livery stable operators, doctors, veterinarians, bankers, implement dealers and garages. The Canadian Pacific Railway began running through the village in 1907 and continued operations until 1988. The first log schoolhouse was built in 1860

Whitechurch

Whitechurch is a village near Lucknow, Ontario, located along the border of Huron and Bruce County. Whitechurch is a residential community, with the Chalmers Presbyterian Church, Whitechurch Community Hall and CMG Building Solutions. The Whitechurch United Church closed on June 24, 2007.

Winthrop

Winthrop is a very small village located on the southeastern part of Huron County, where two county roads, Winthrop and Kippen (N Line), meet. Winthrop has a few shops, a general store, and a post office.

Lucknow

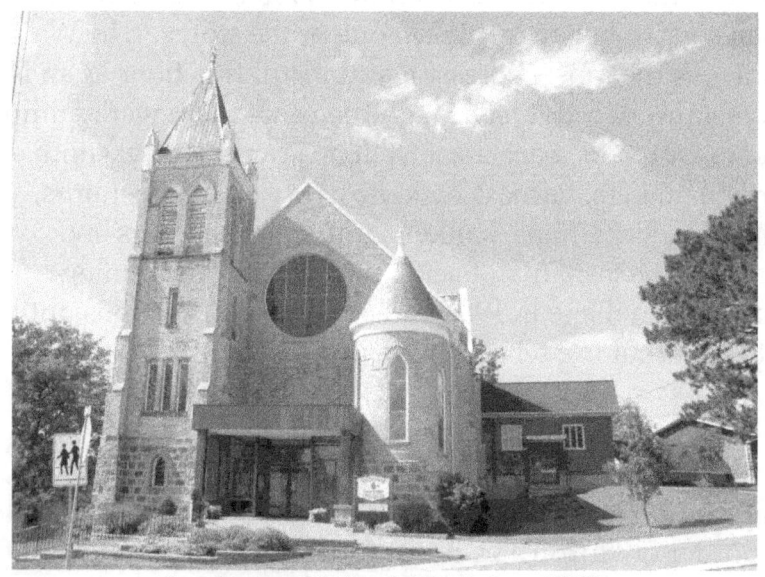

Lucknow United Church – 1885
Havelock Street

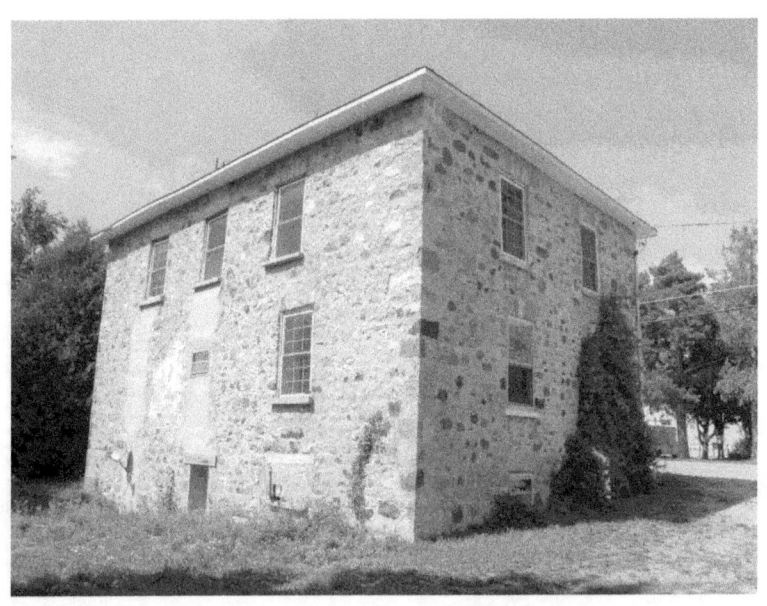

Multi-coloured stone two-storey farmhouse

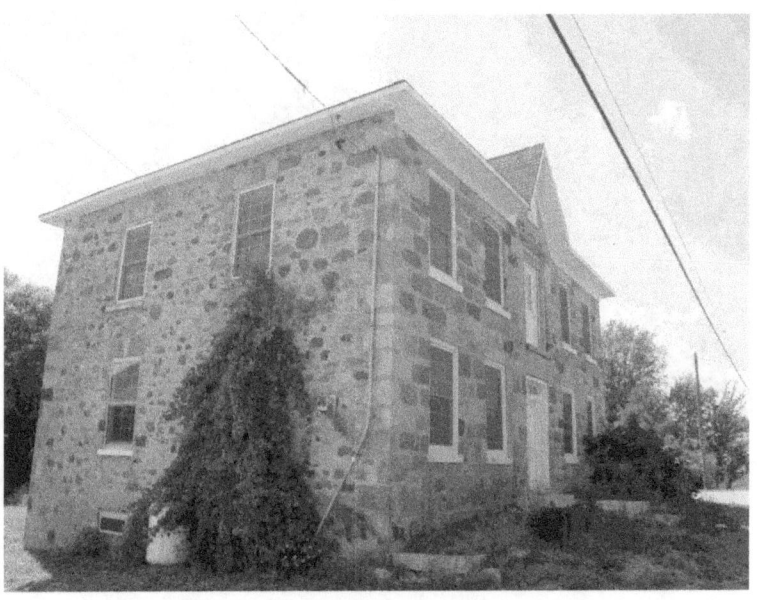

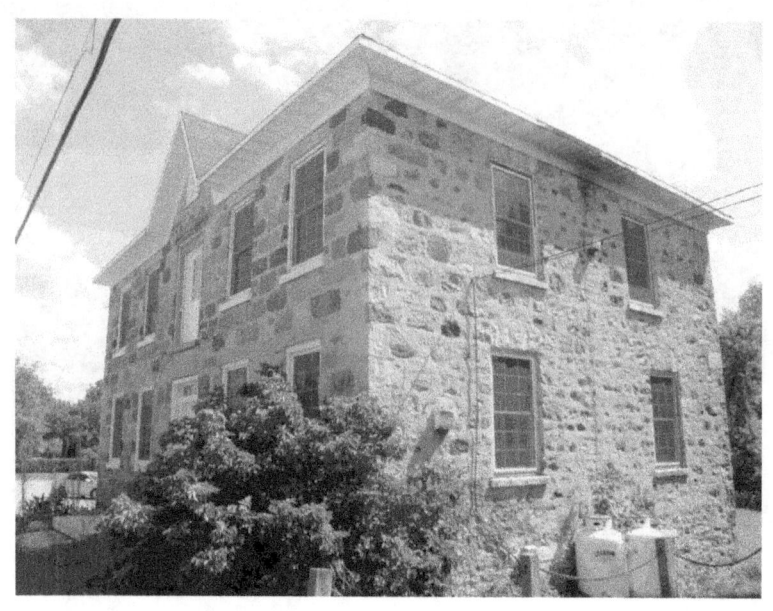

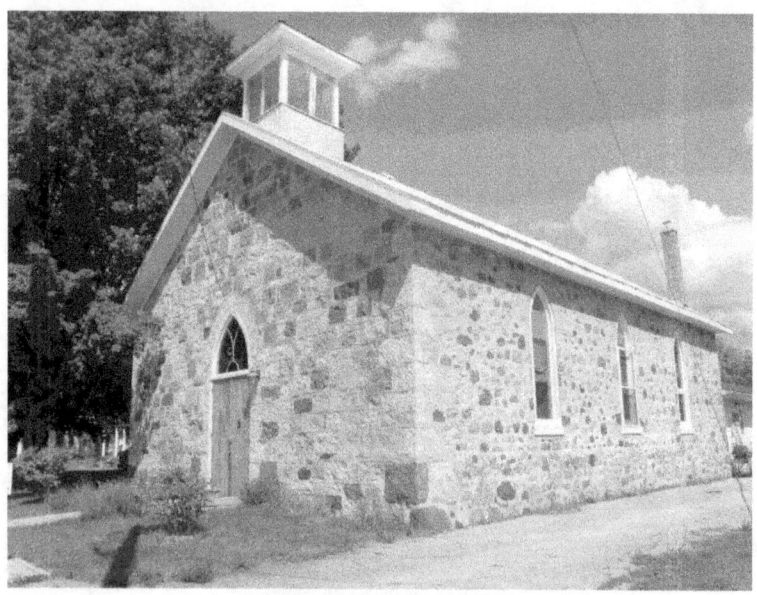

I.H.S. Church - 1873

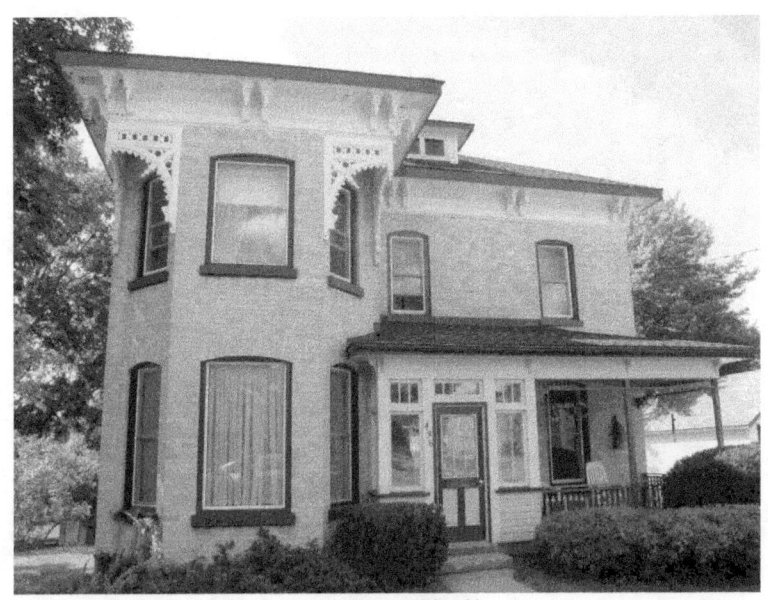

436 Campbell
Paired cornice brackets, fancy latticework

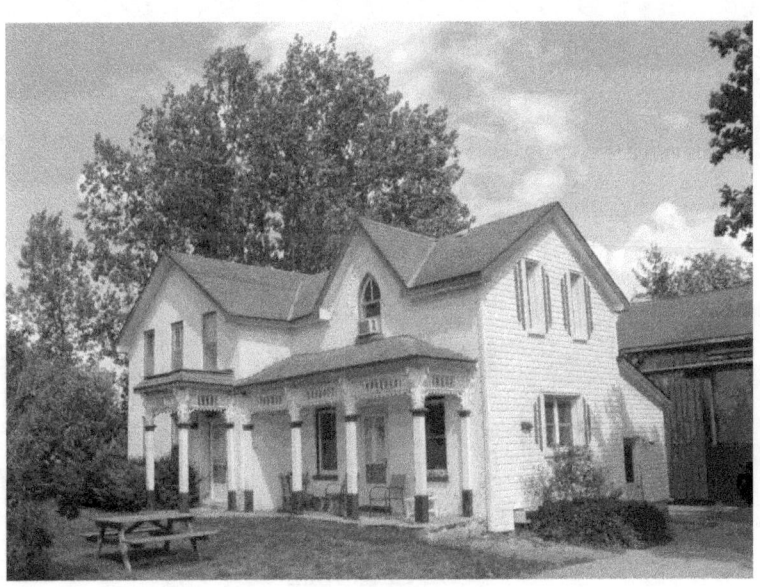

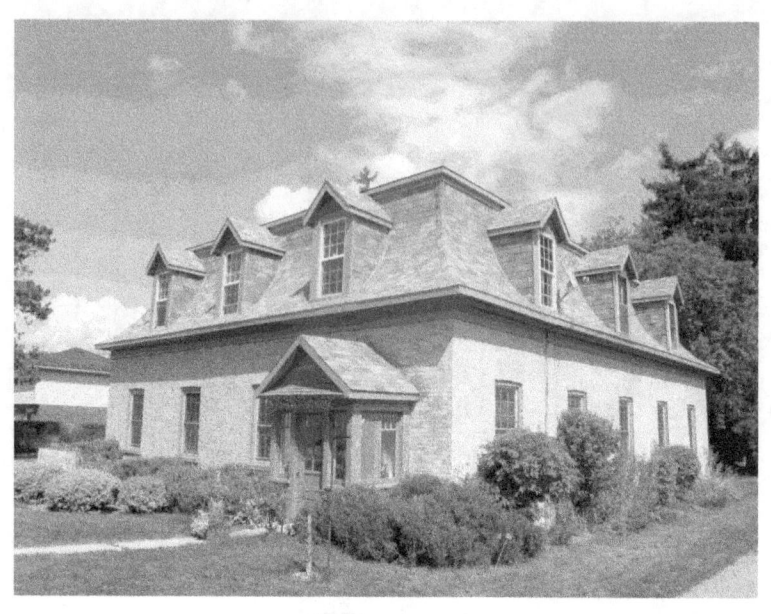

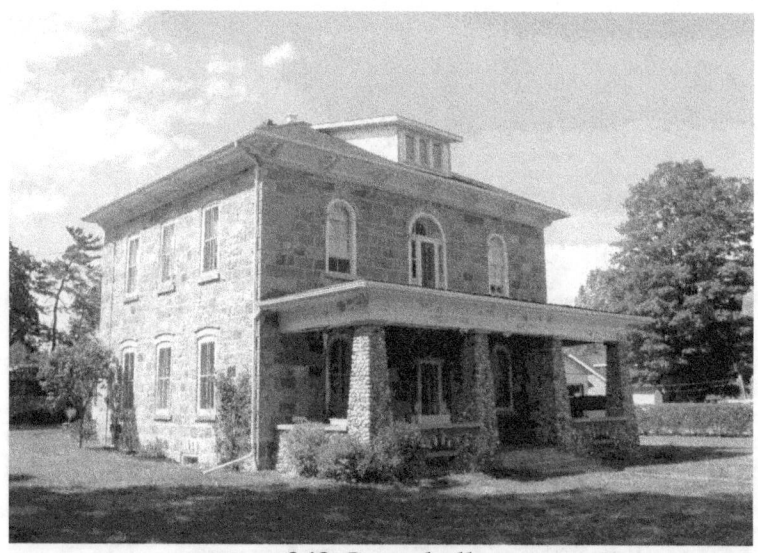

362 Campbell
Multi-coloured stone, paired cornice brackets

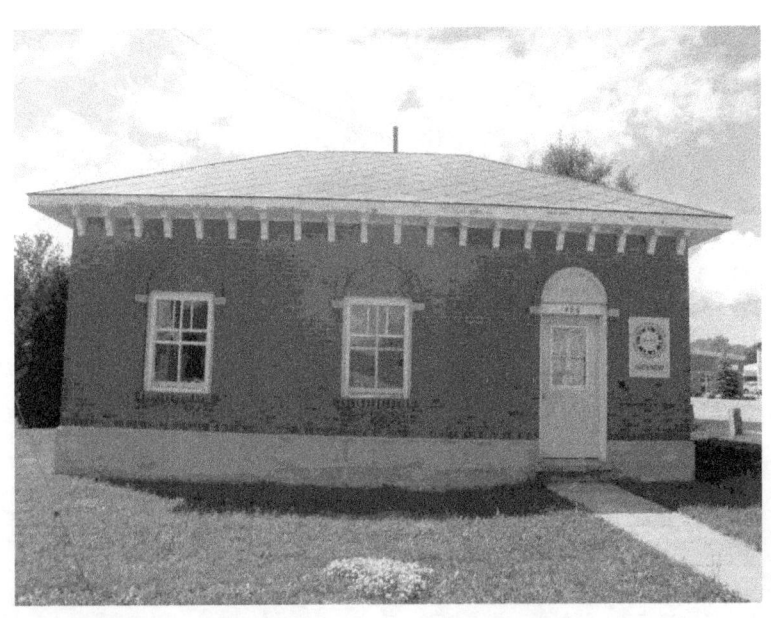

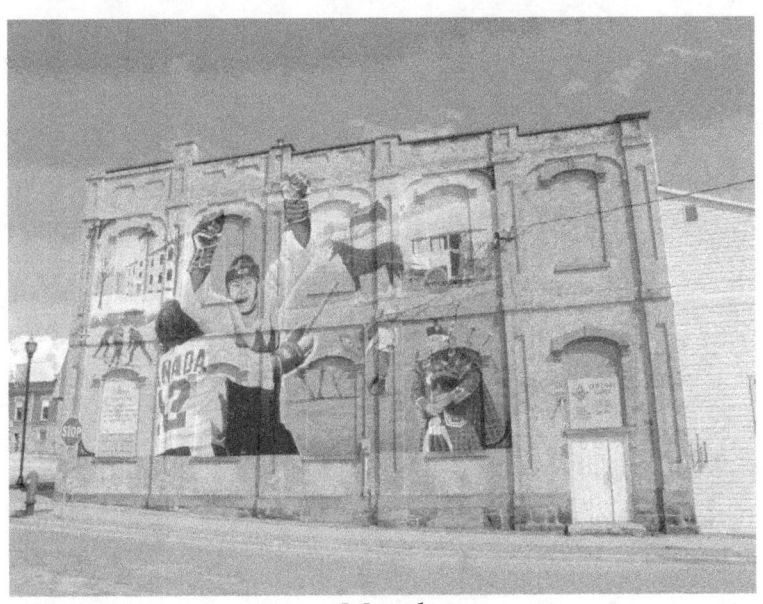

Mural

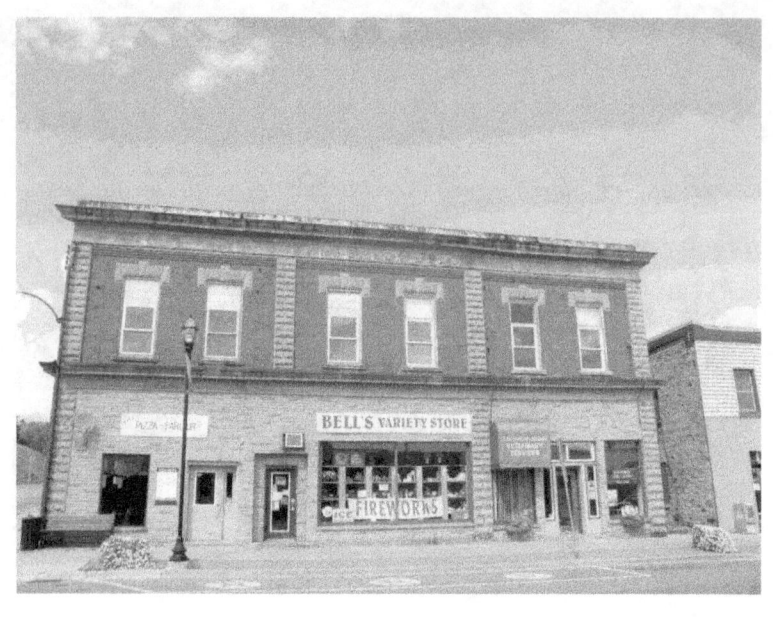

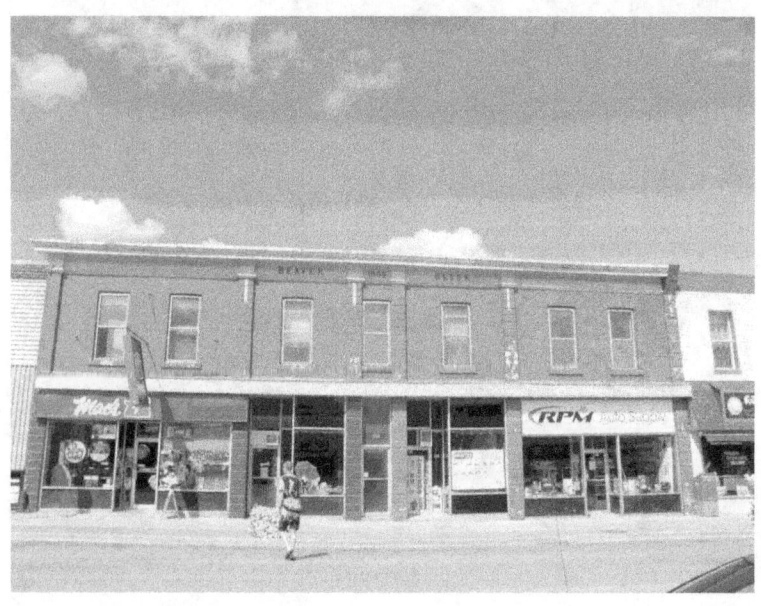

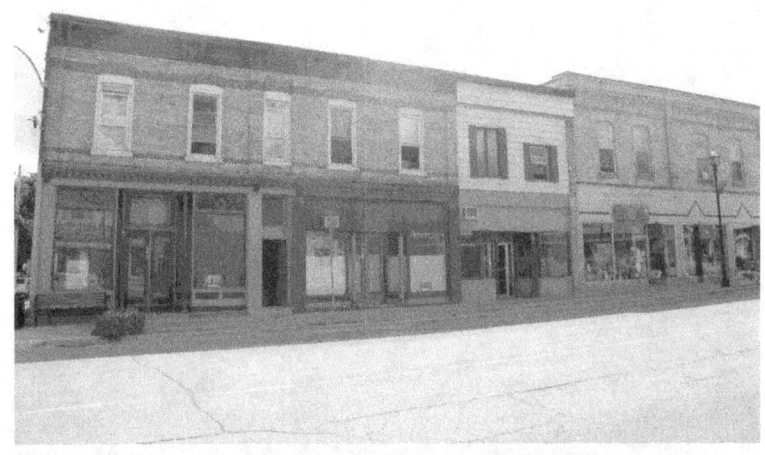

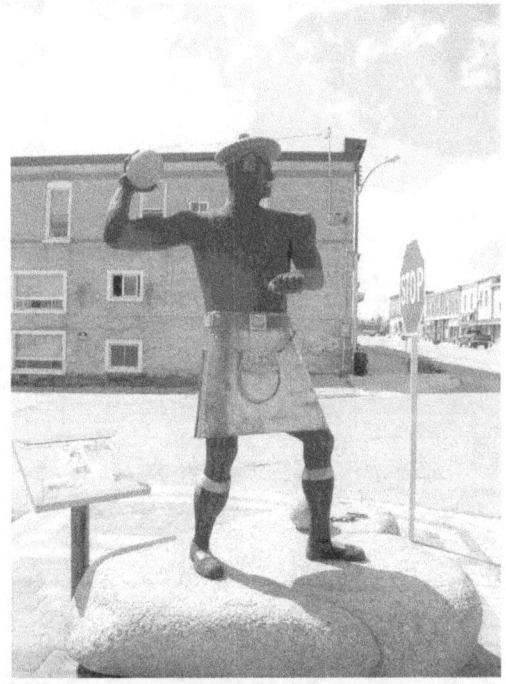

Donald Dinnie, a Scottish athlete known for his incredible strength, competed at many Caledonian Games held in Lucknow in the late 19th century.

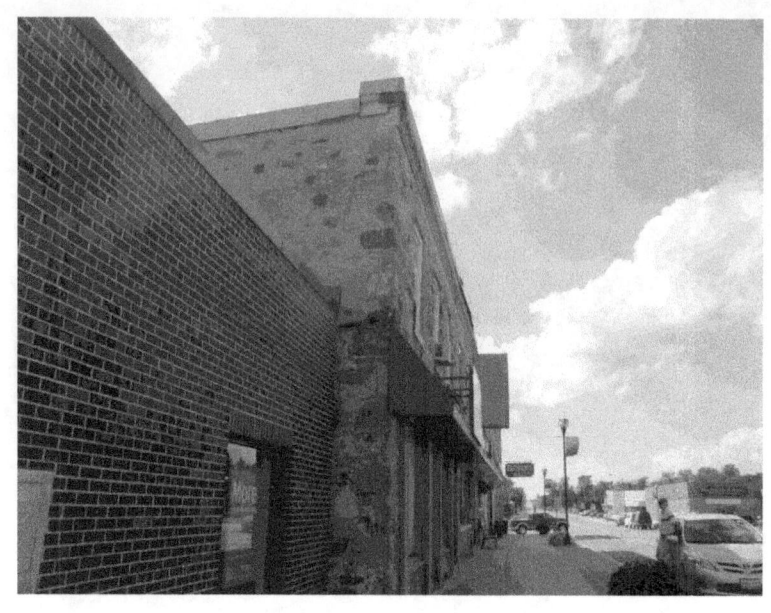

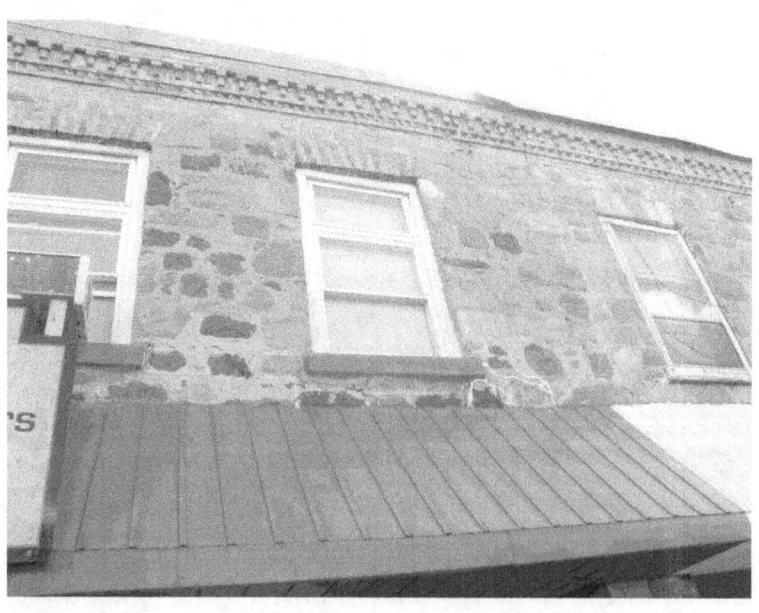

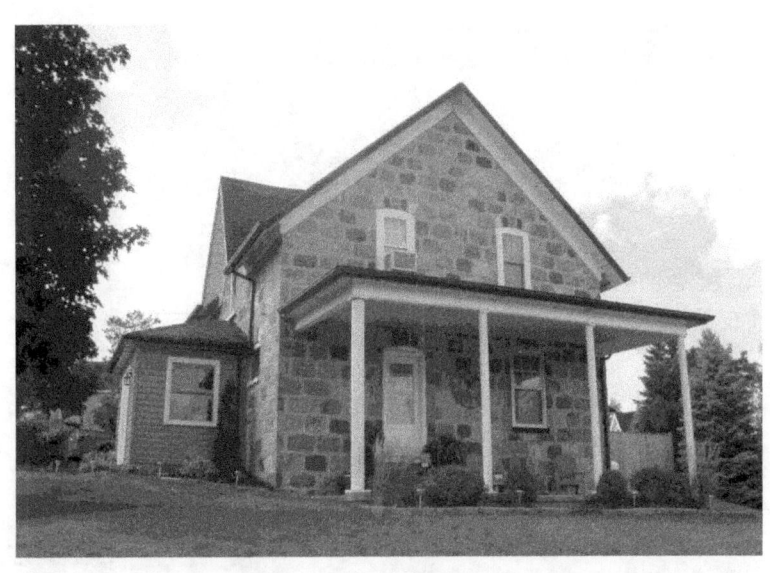

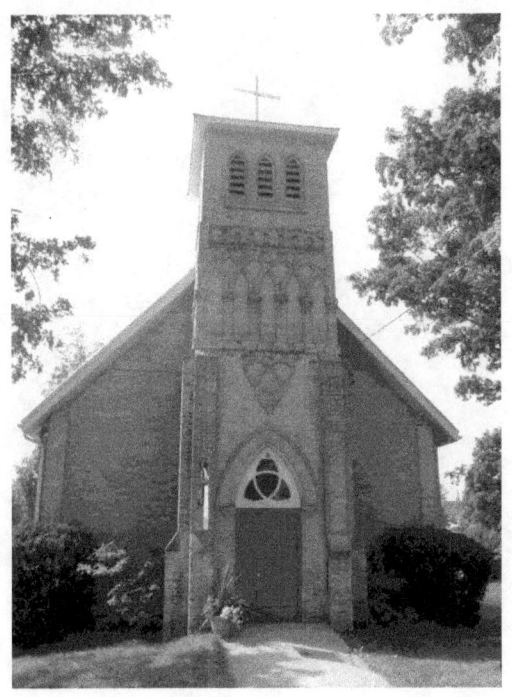

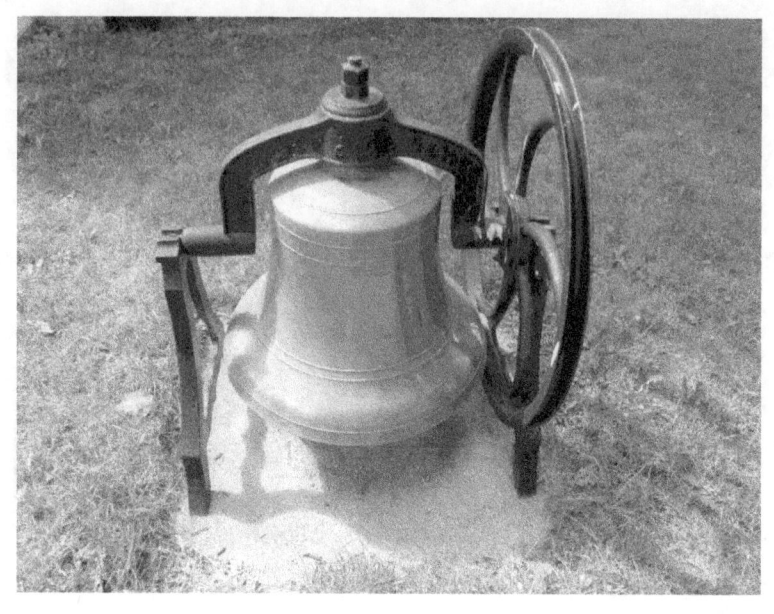

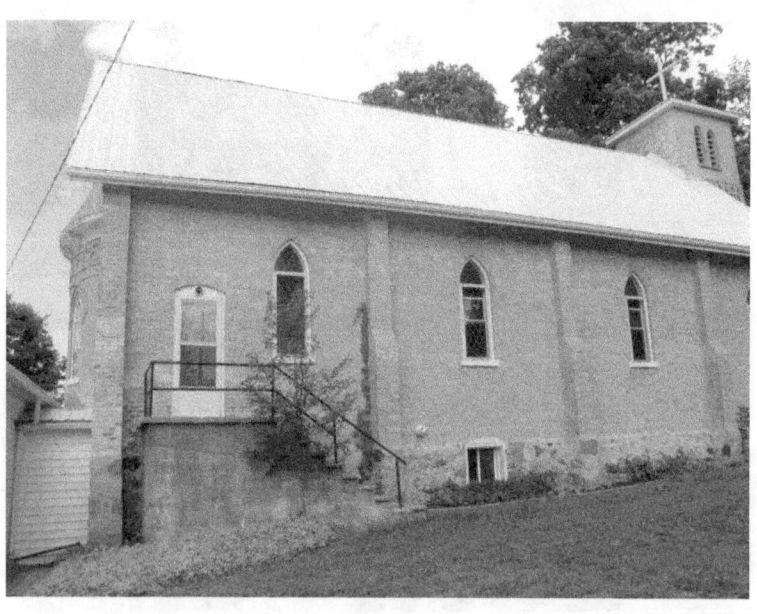

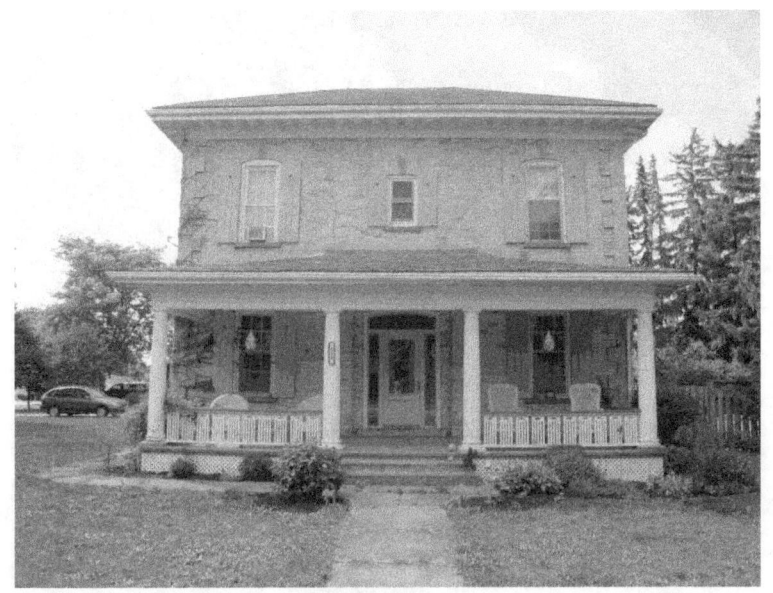

#638
Outram Street

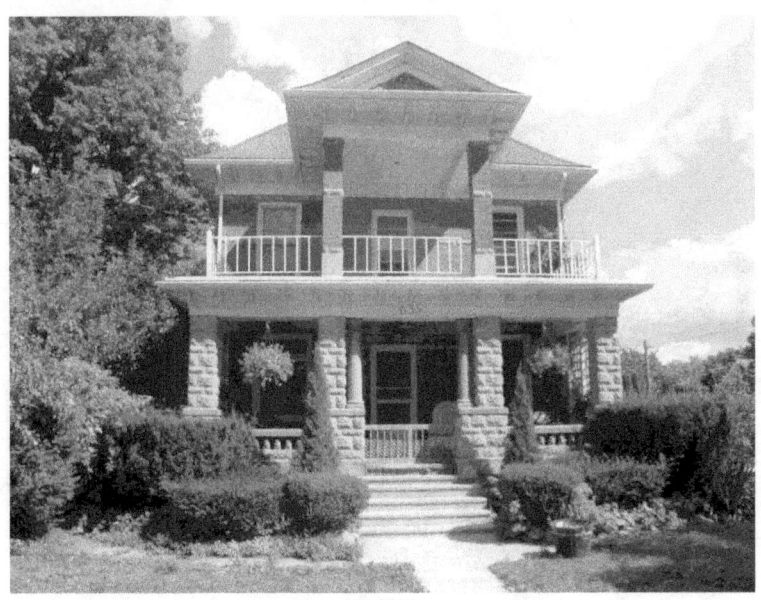

#635

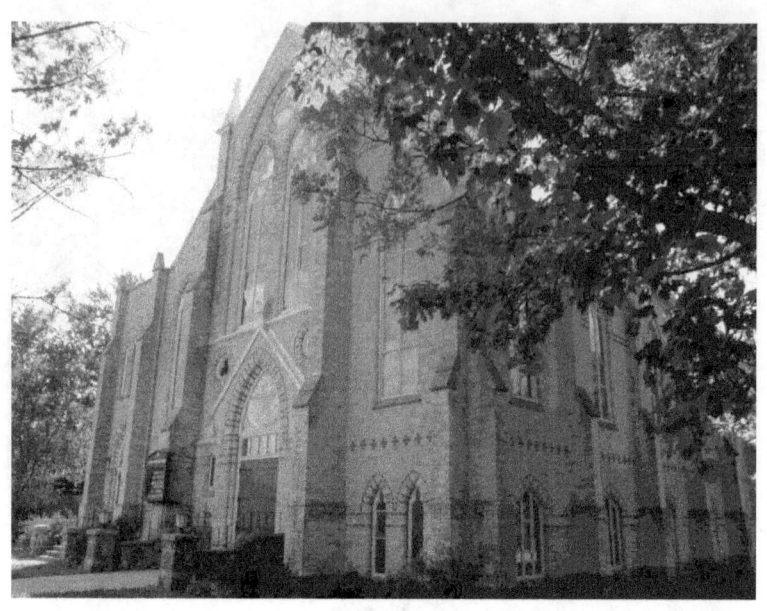

Lucknow Presbyterian Church – established 1889

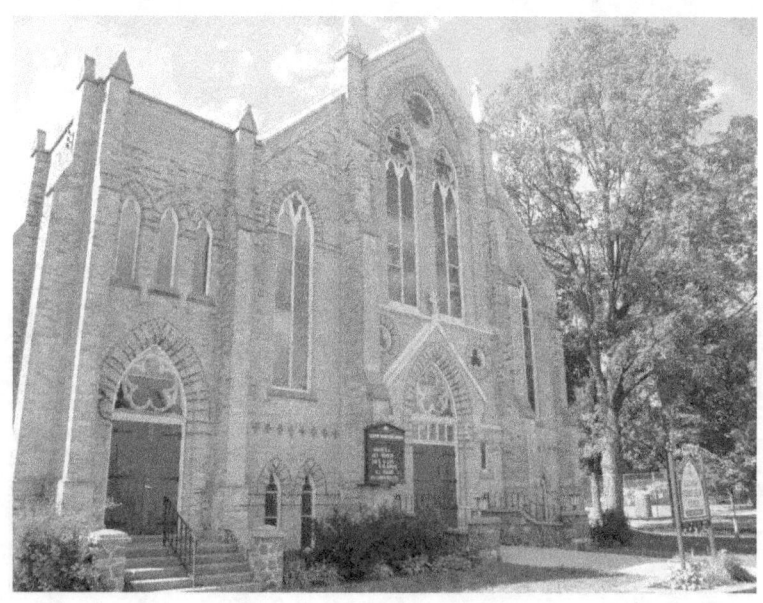

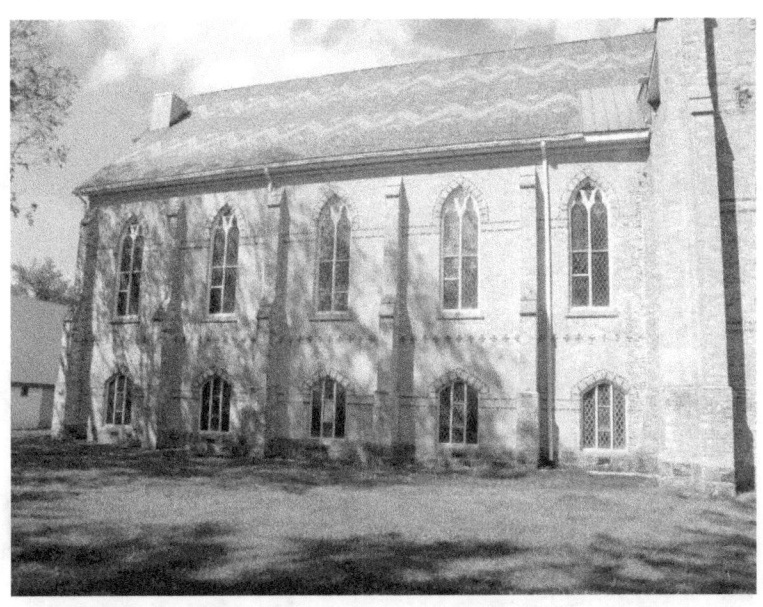

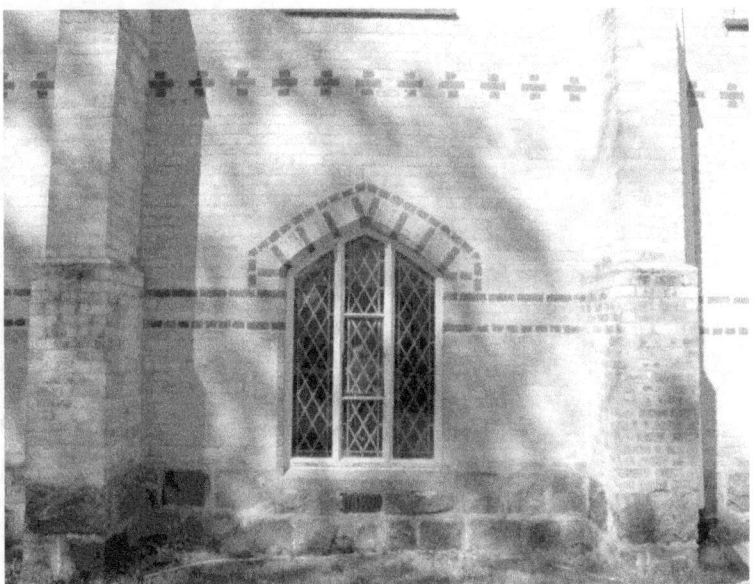

Dublin

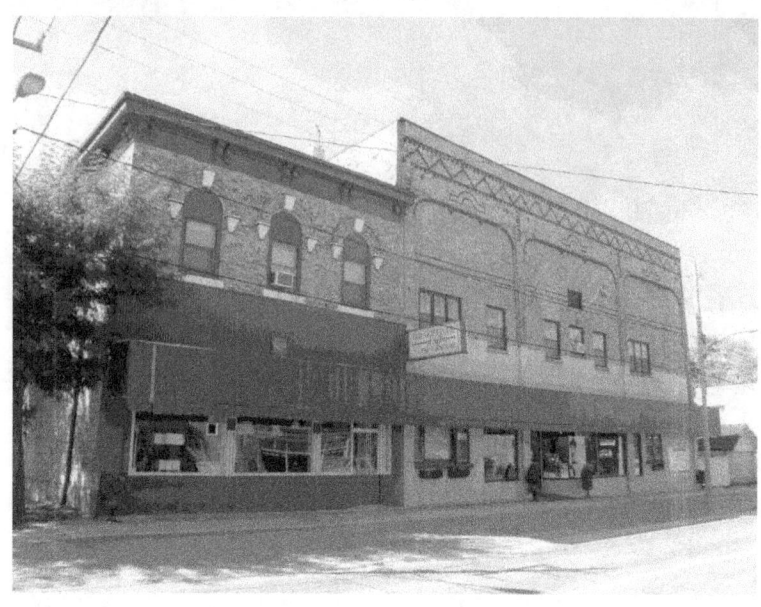

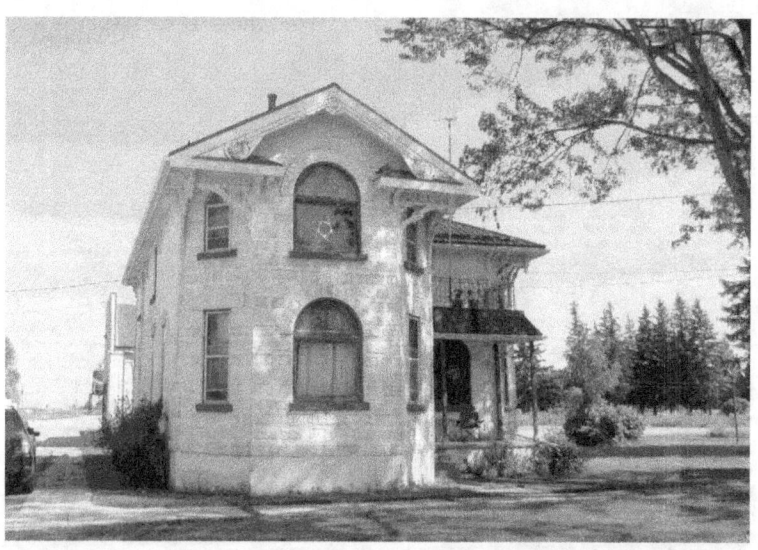

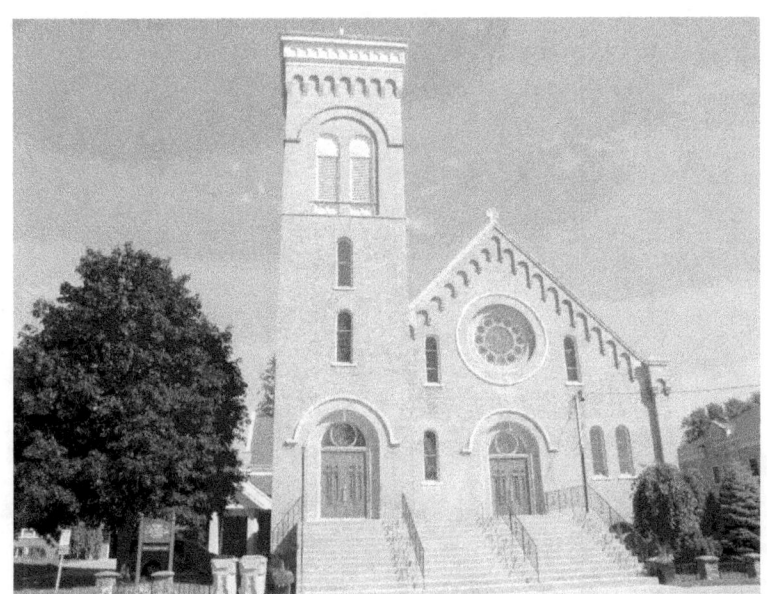

St. Patrick's Catholic Church, Dublin

Mitchell

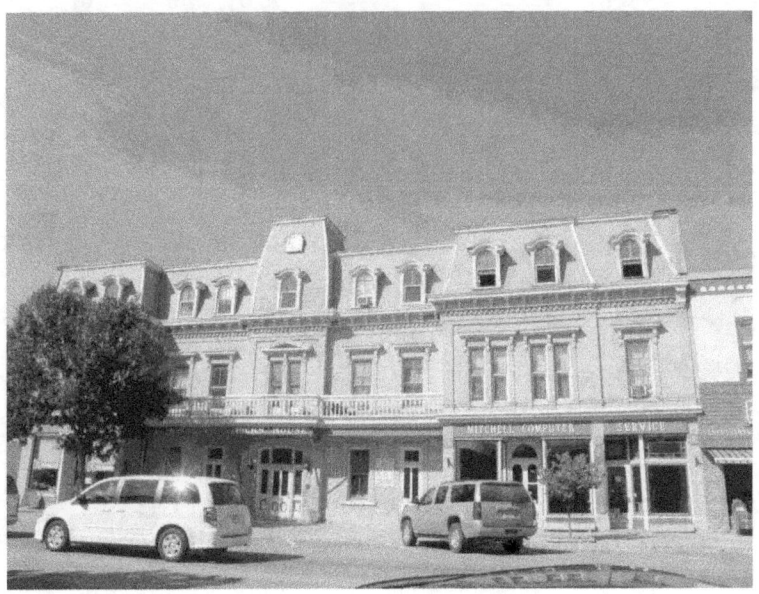

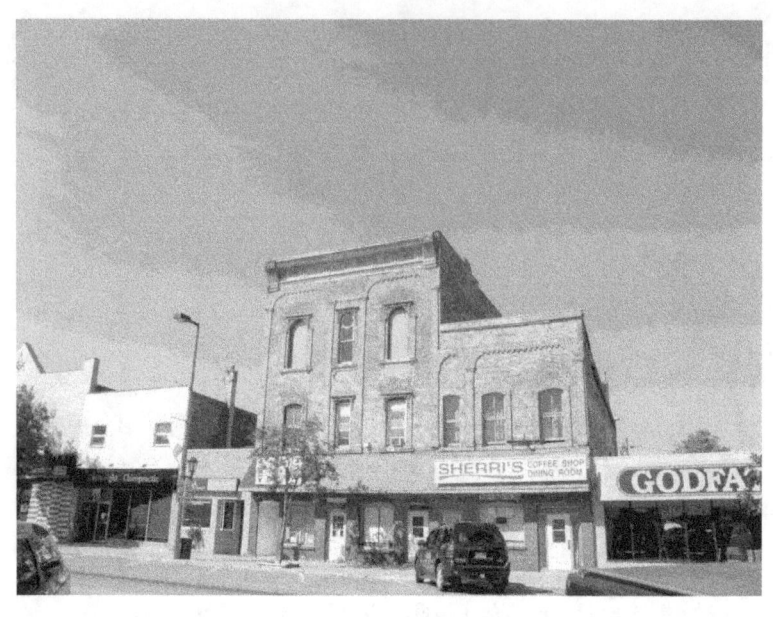

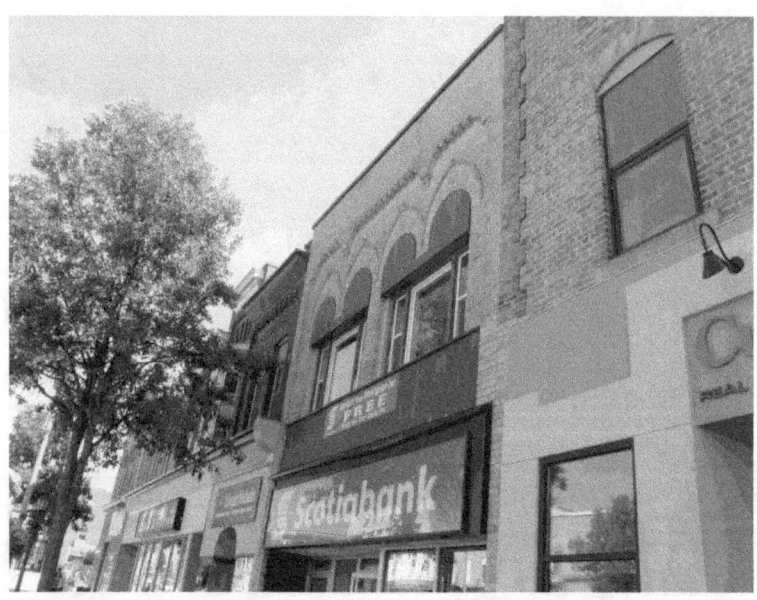

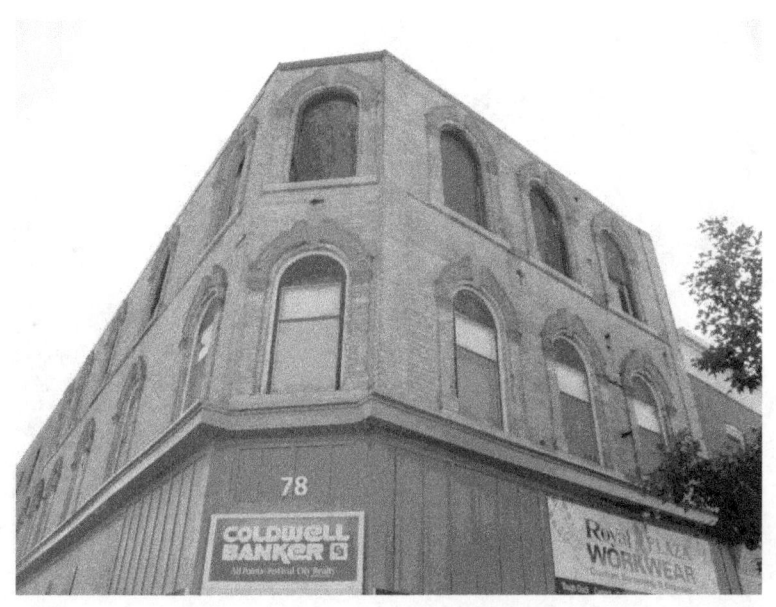

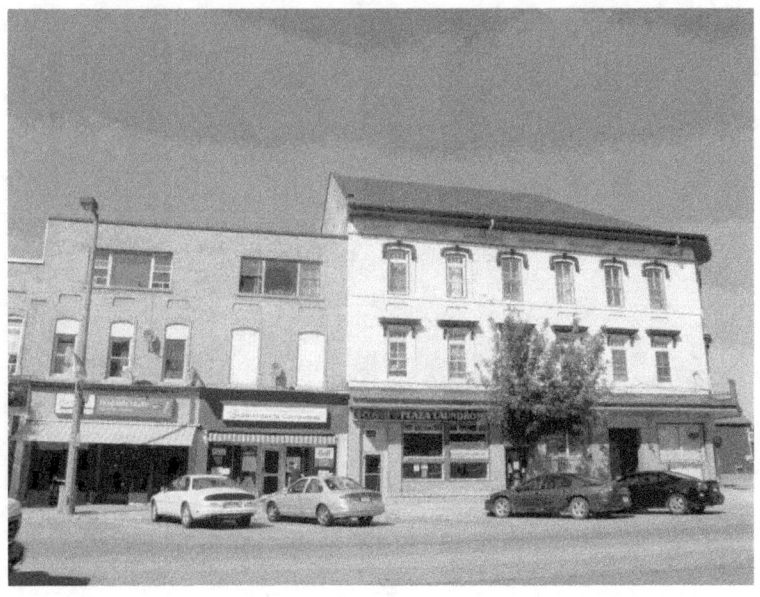

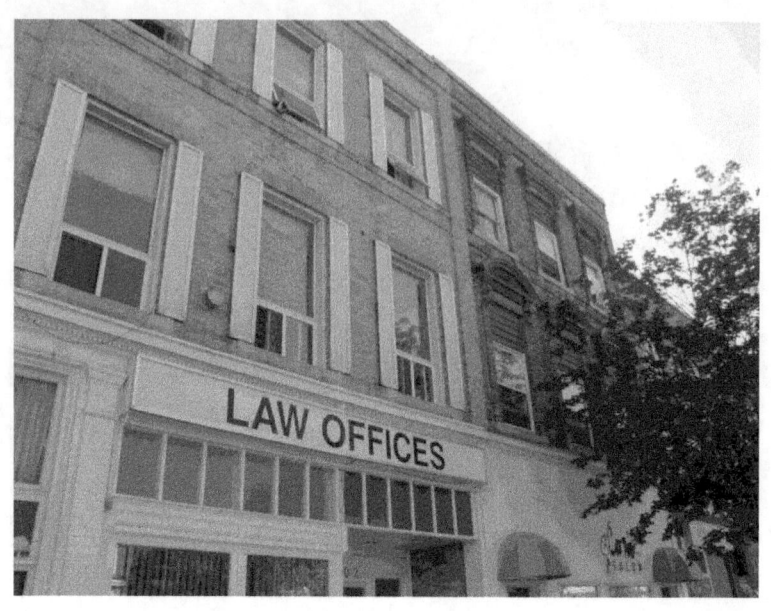

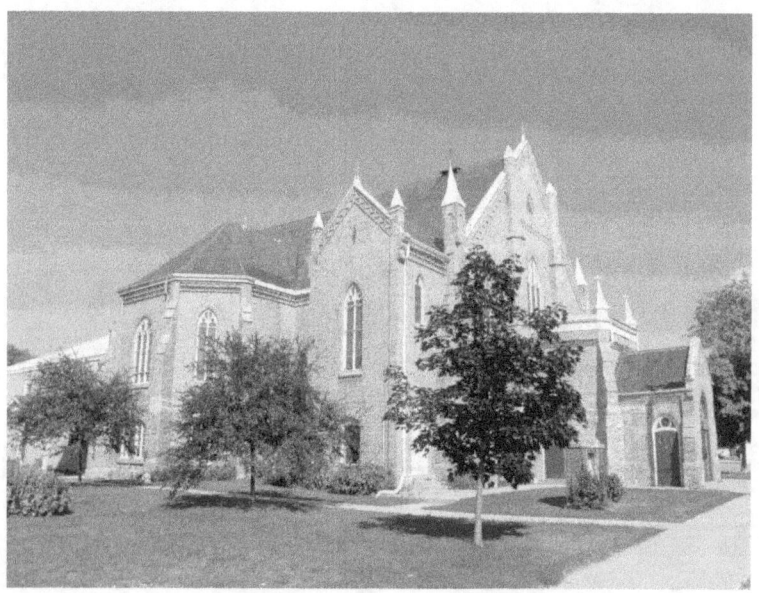

Main Street United Church

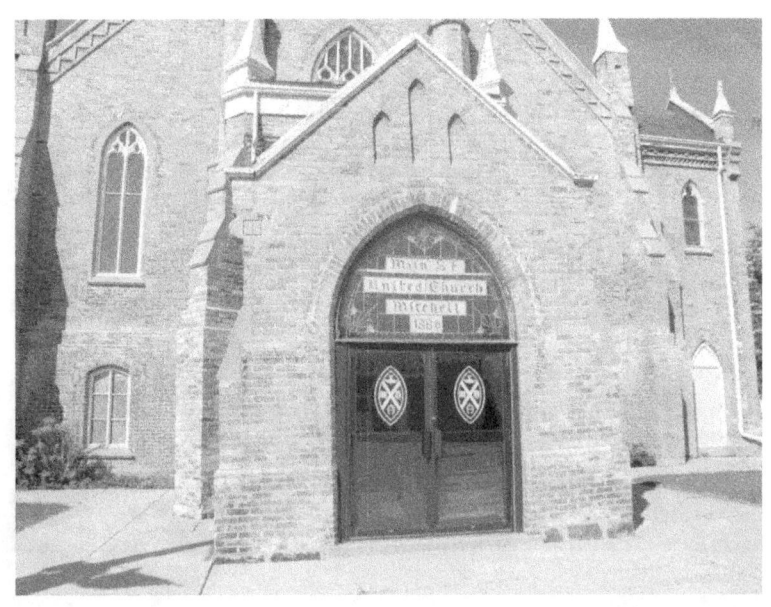

Main Street United Church, Mitchell - 1886

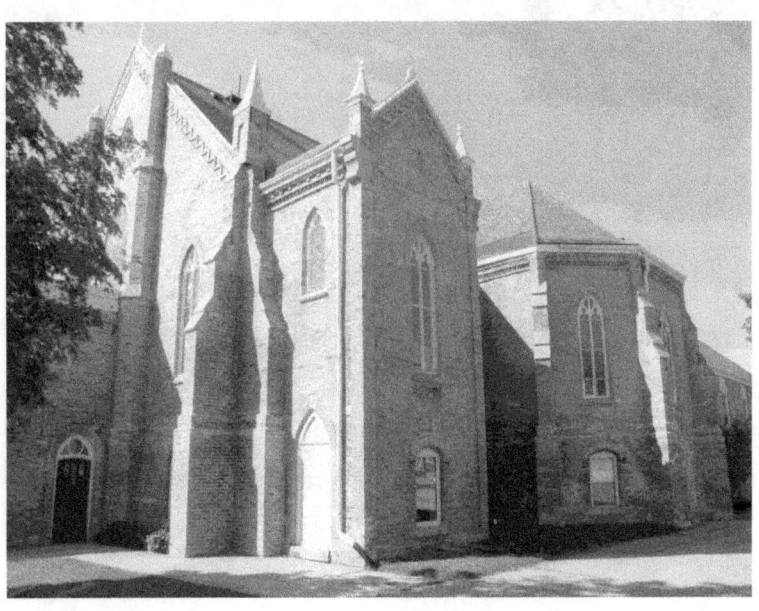

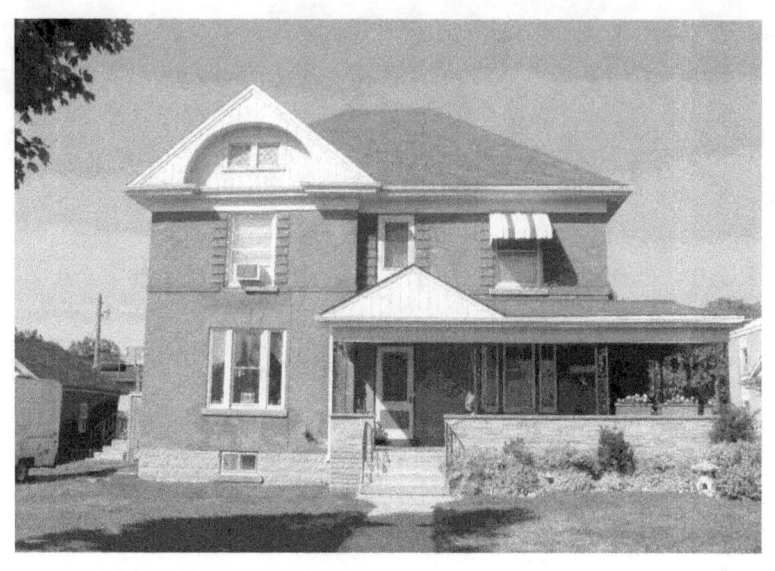

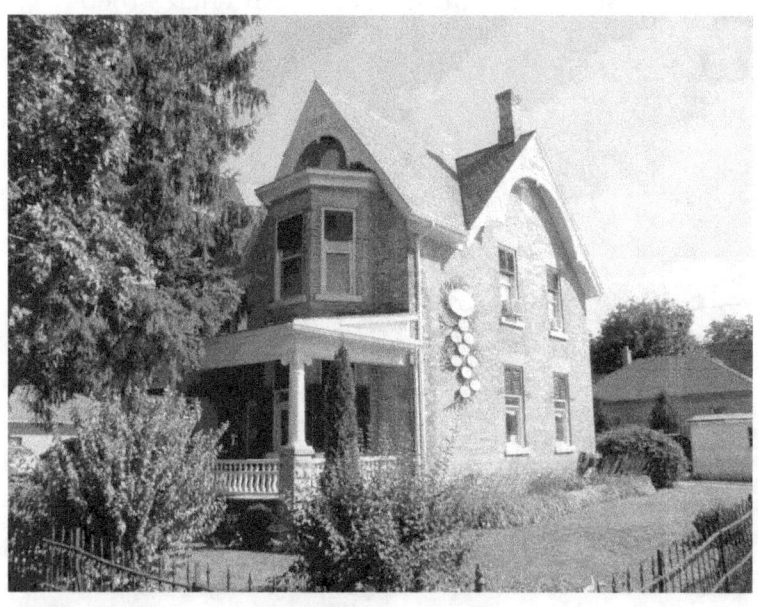

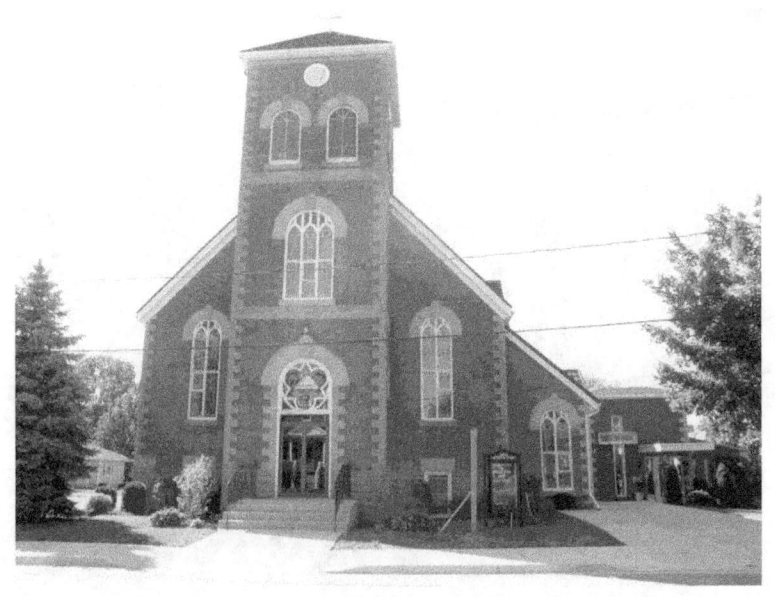

Grace Lutheran Church – erected A.D. 1913

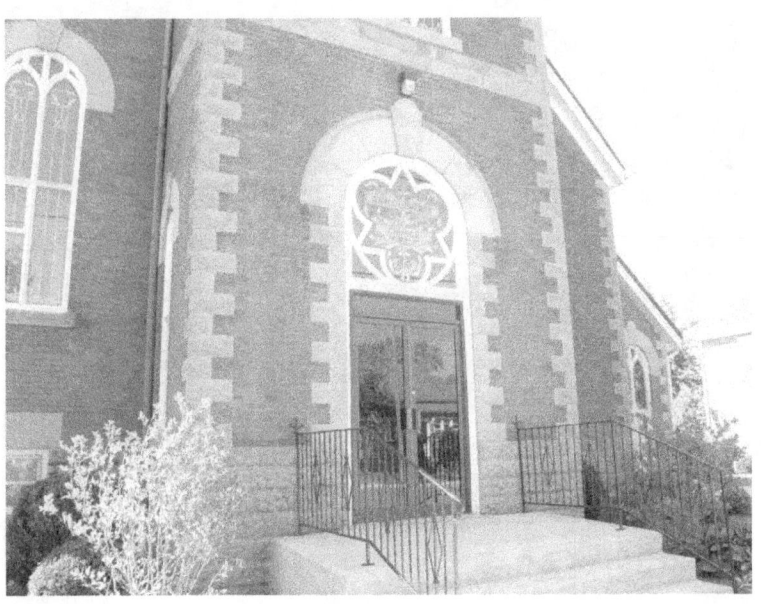

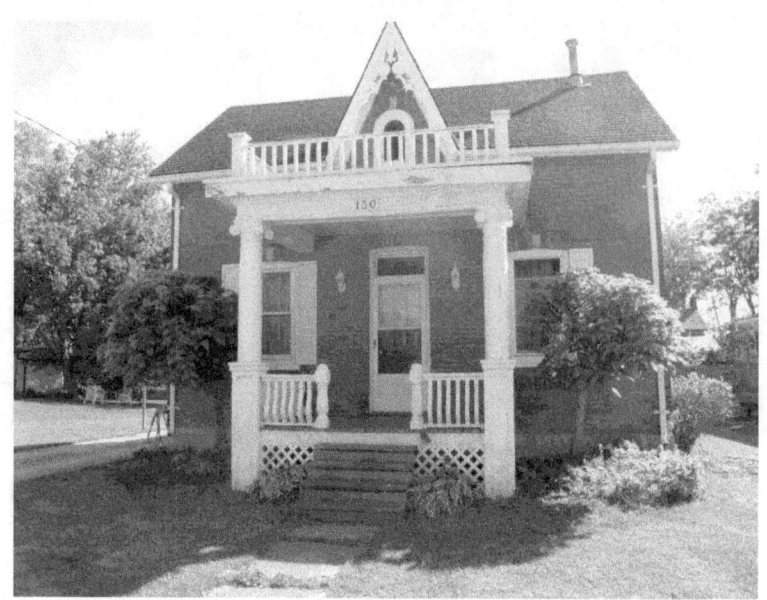

#130

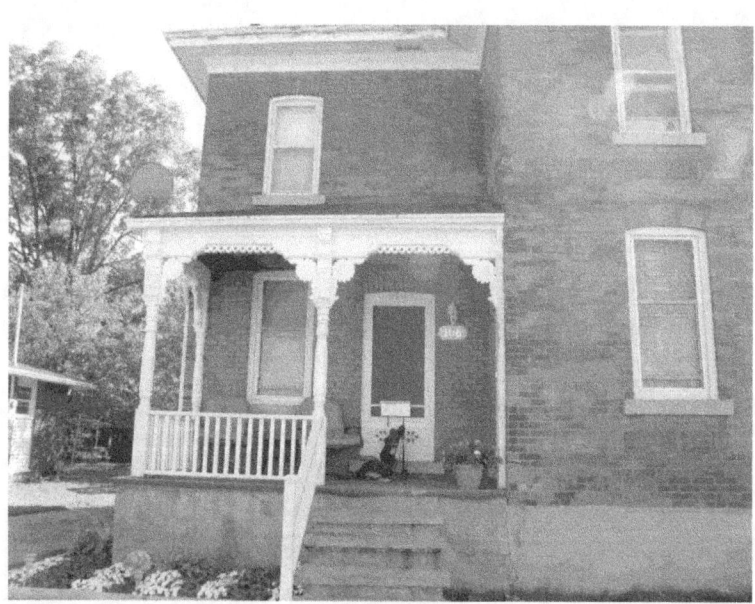

#106

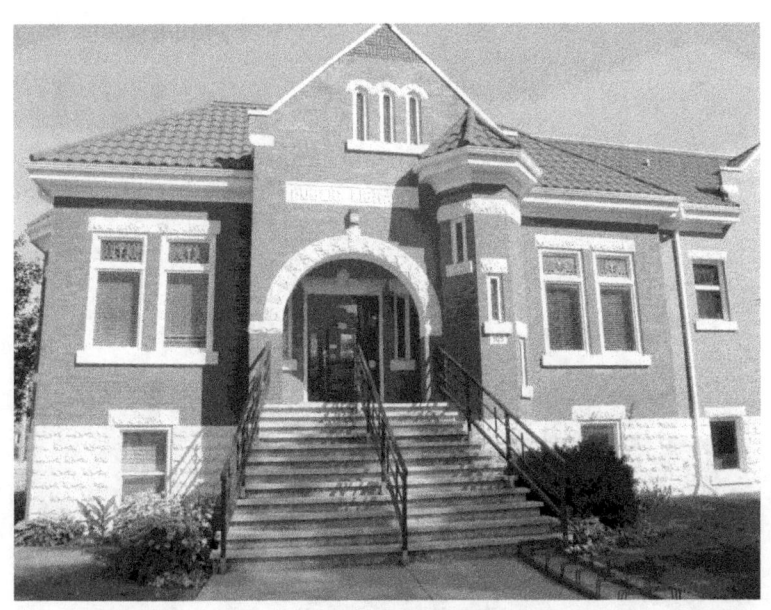

West Perth Public Library

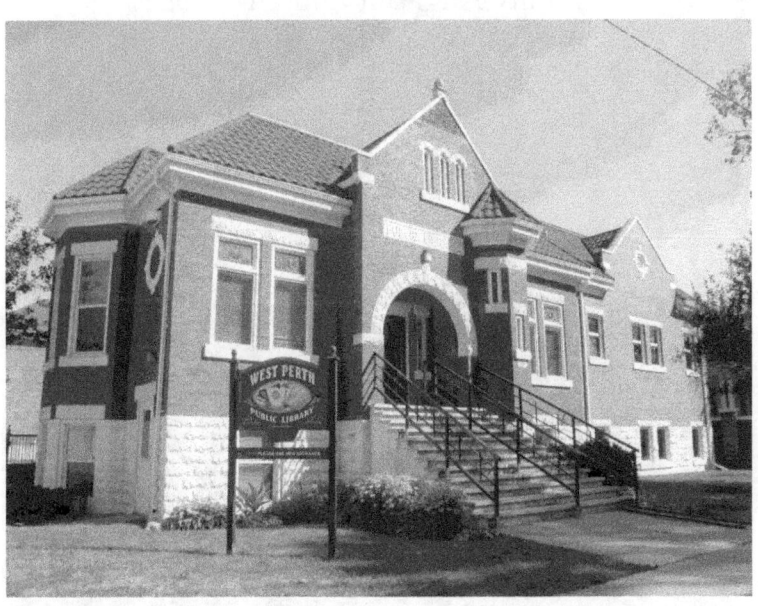

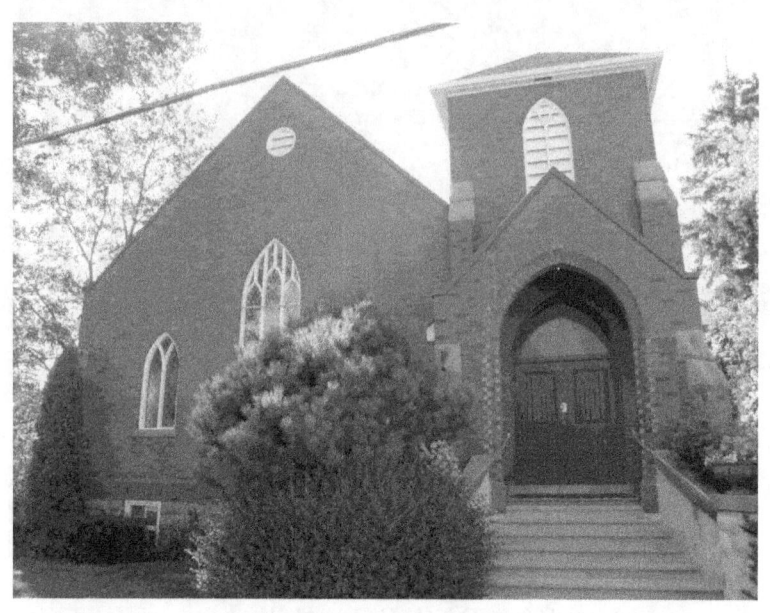

Trinity Anglican Church - 1858

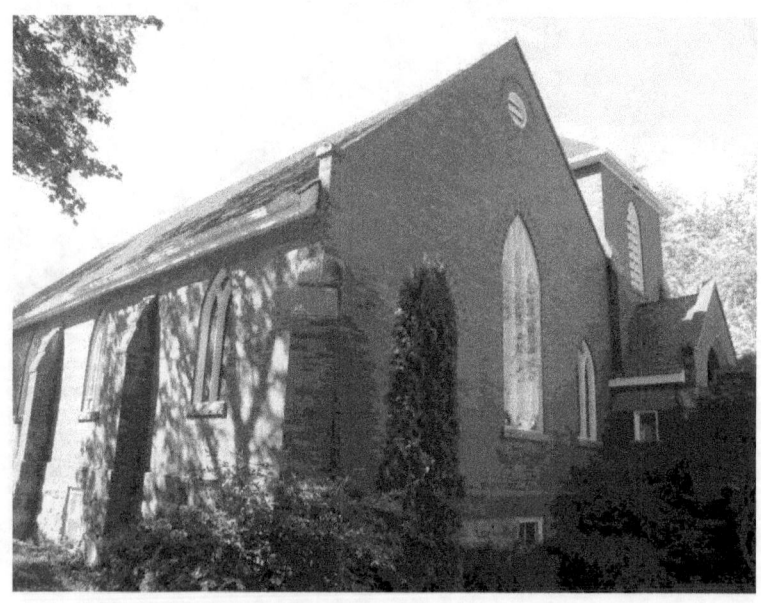

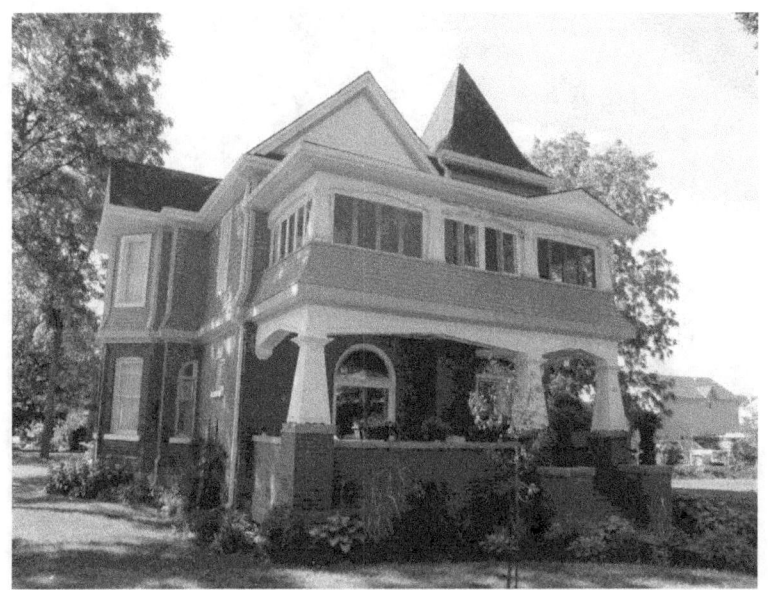

#100

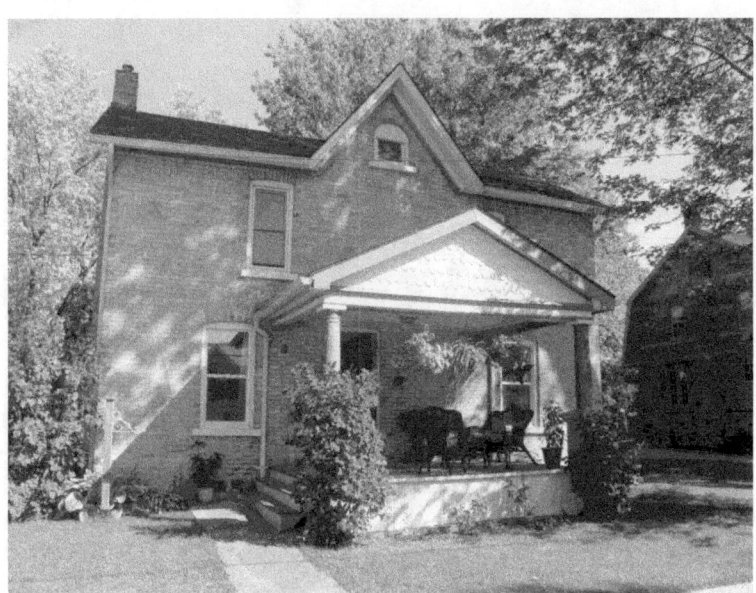

97 St. Andrew Street

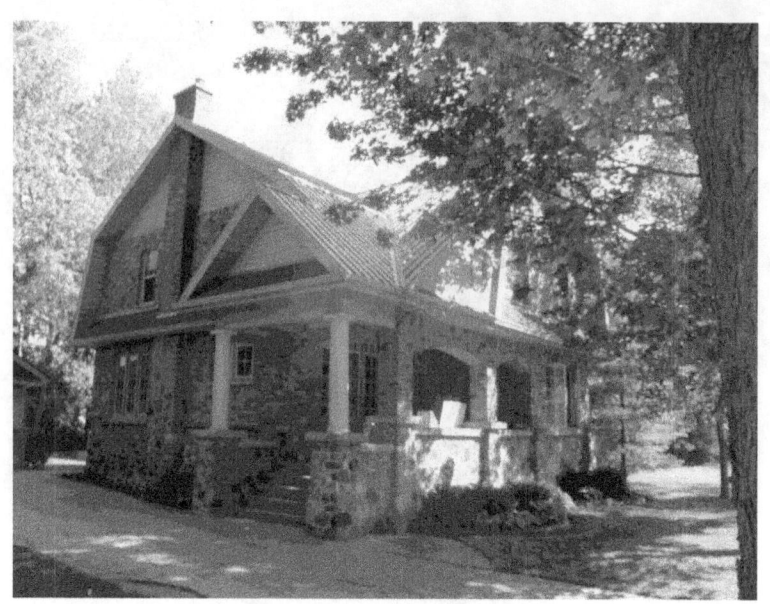

95 St. Andrew Street

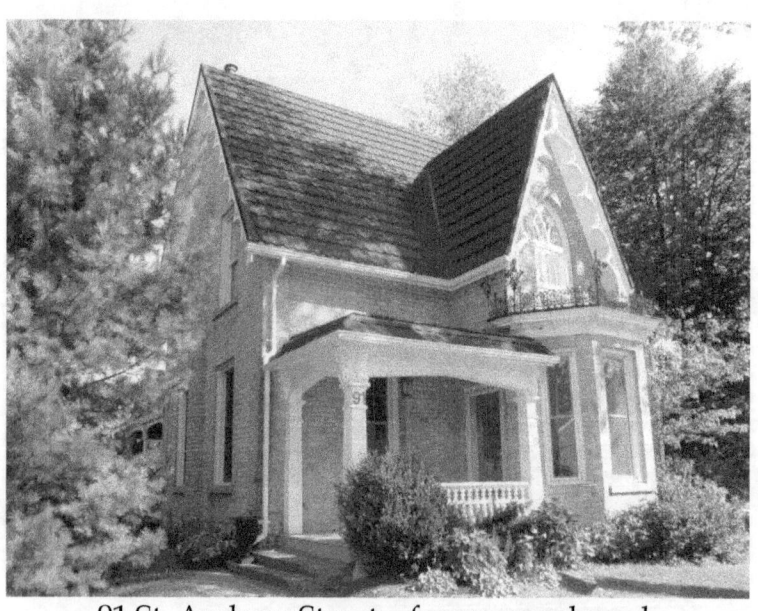

91 St. Andrew Street – fancy vergeboard,
Iron work above bay window

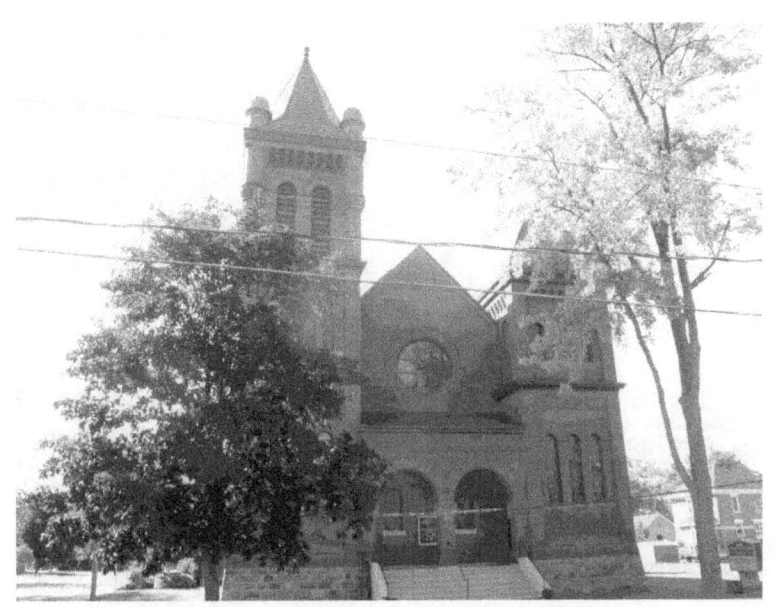

Knox Presbyterian Church, 92 Main Street

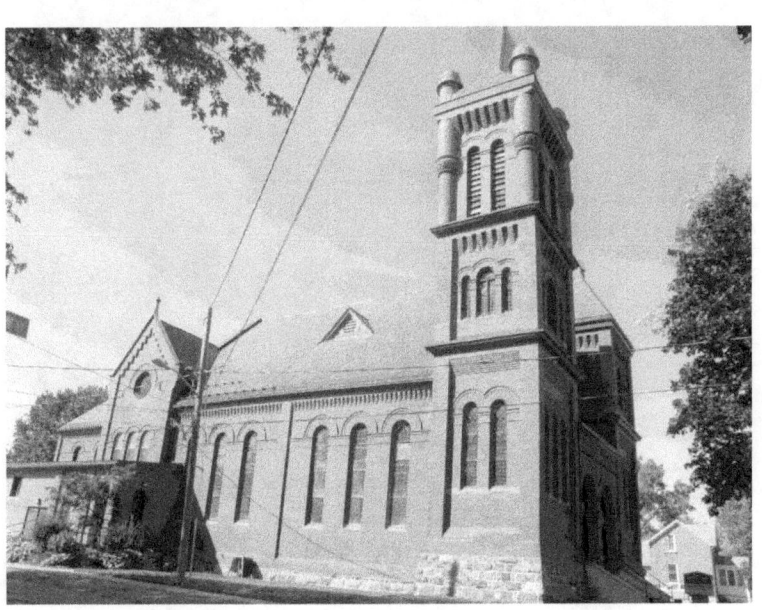

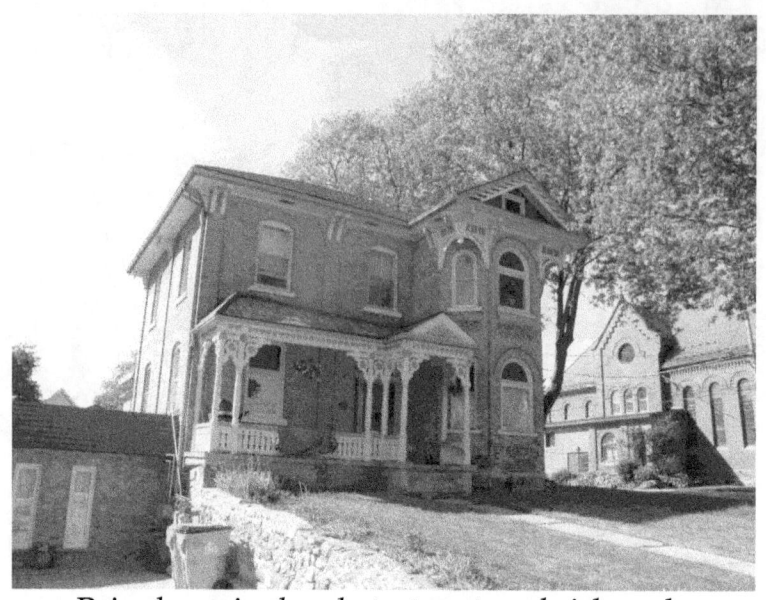

Paired cornice brackets, two-tone brickwork, fancy lattice work

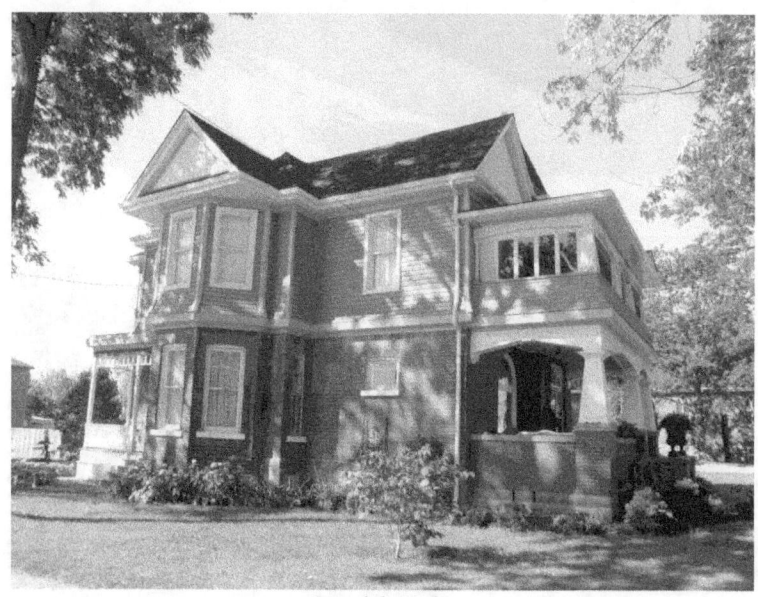

Red brick

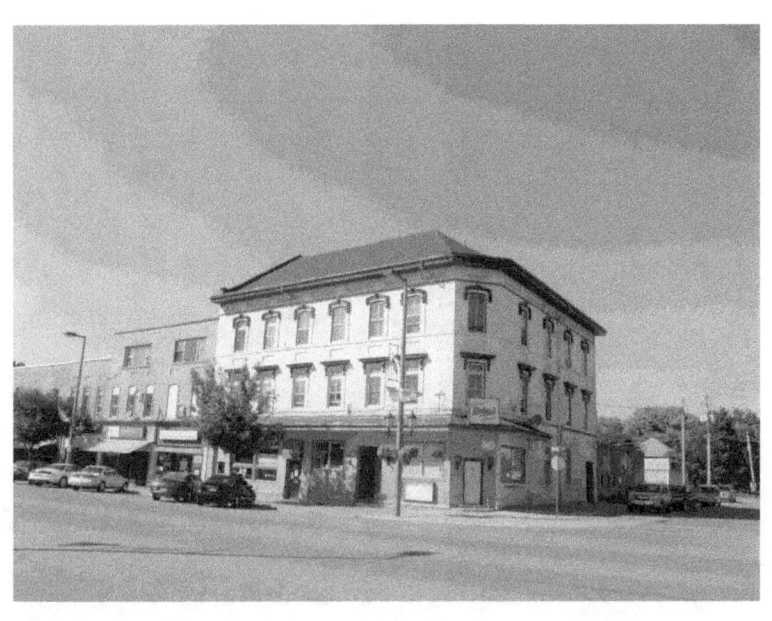

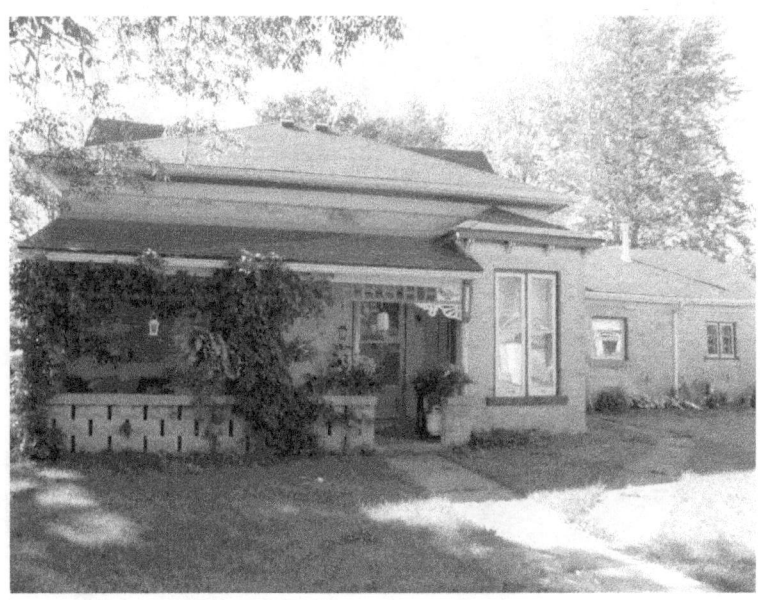

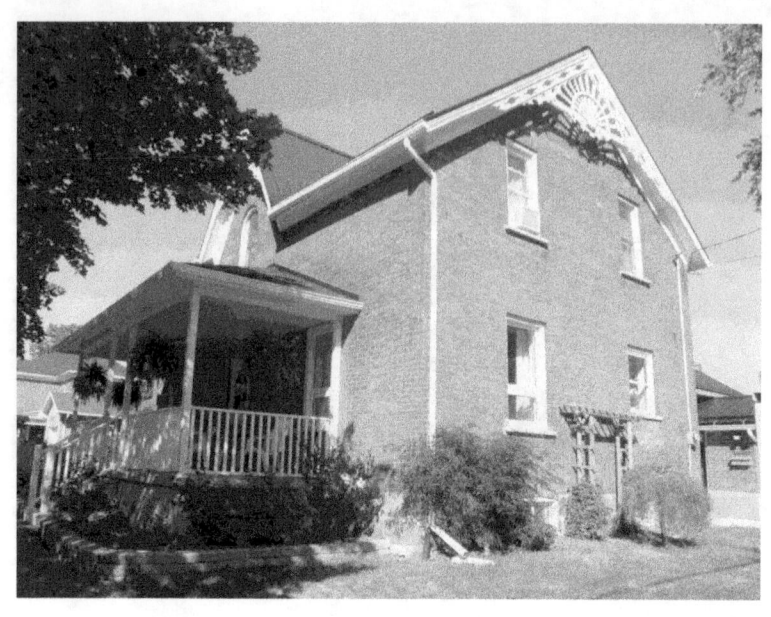

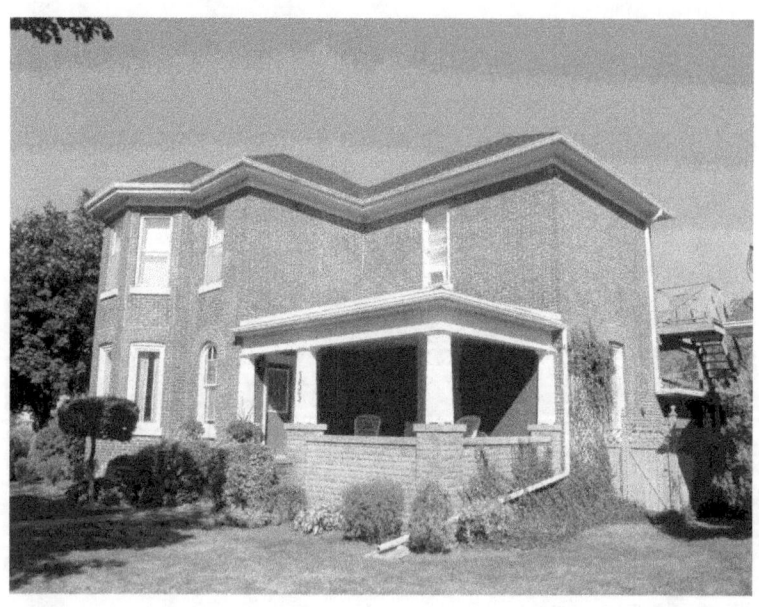

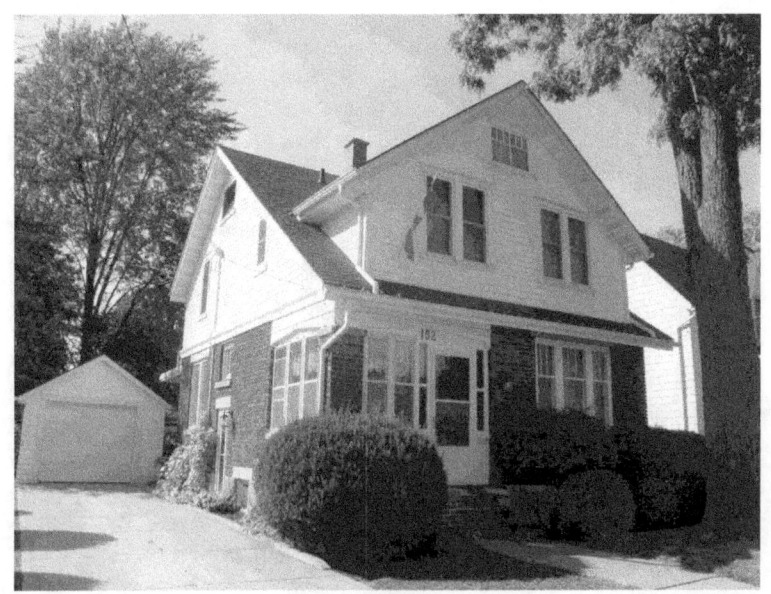

#152

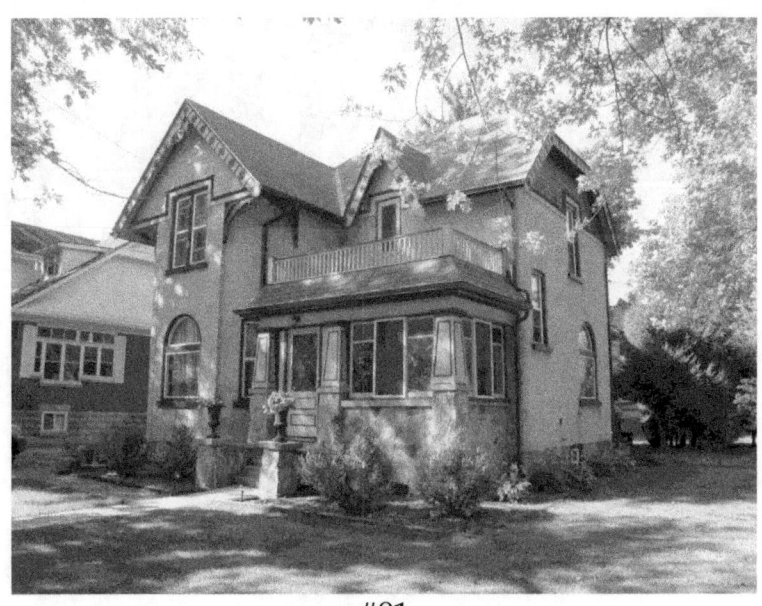

#91

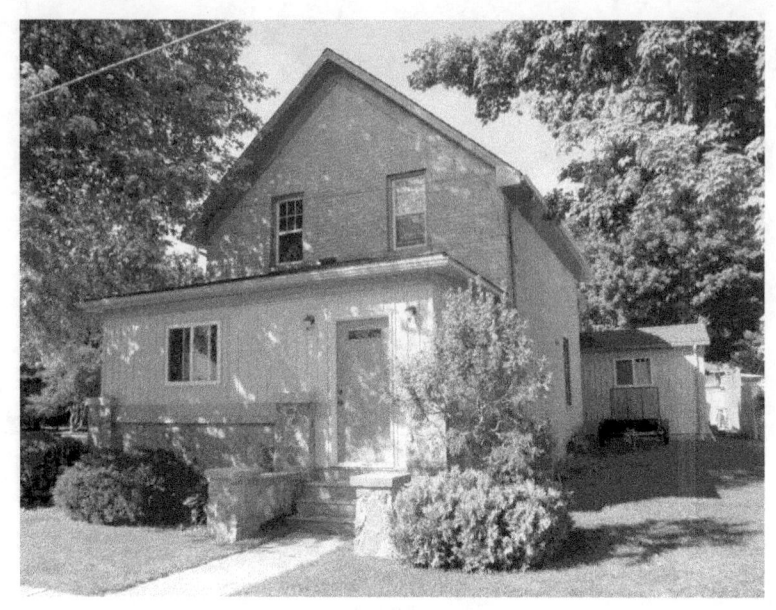

Waterloo Street

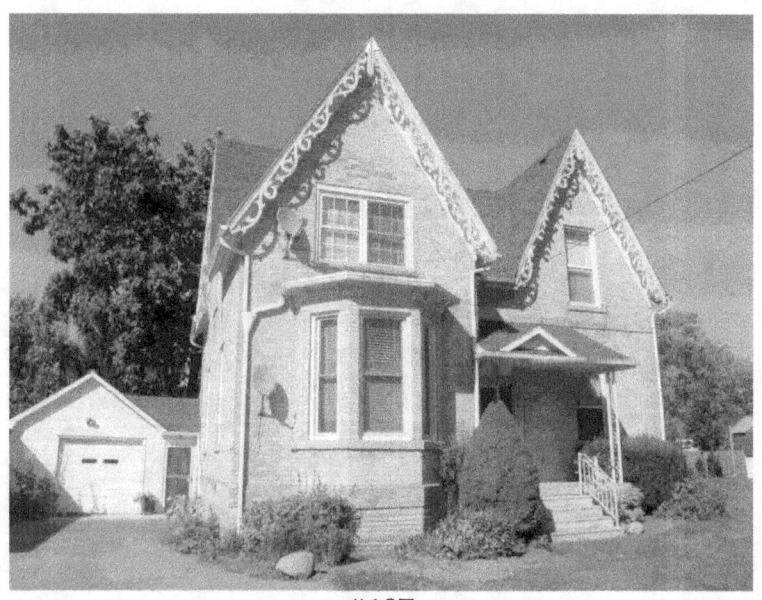

#107

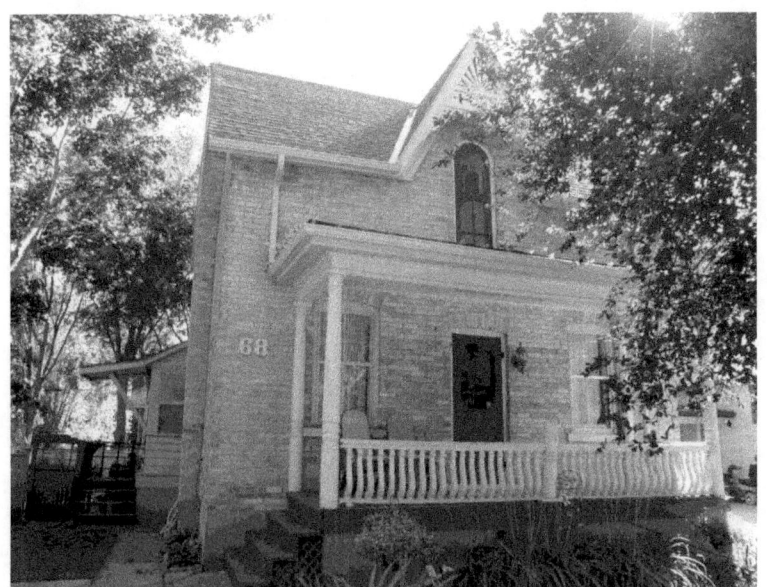

#68

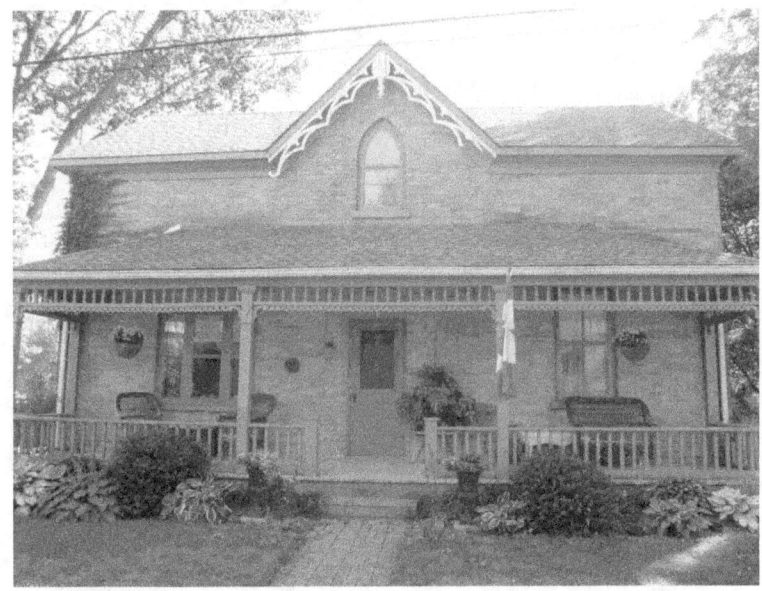

#38 – two-tone bricks, fancy vergeboard on arch

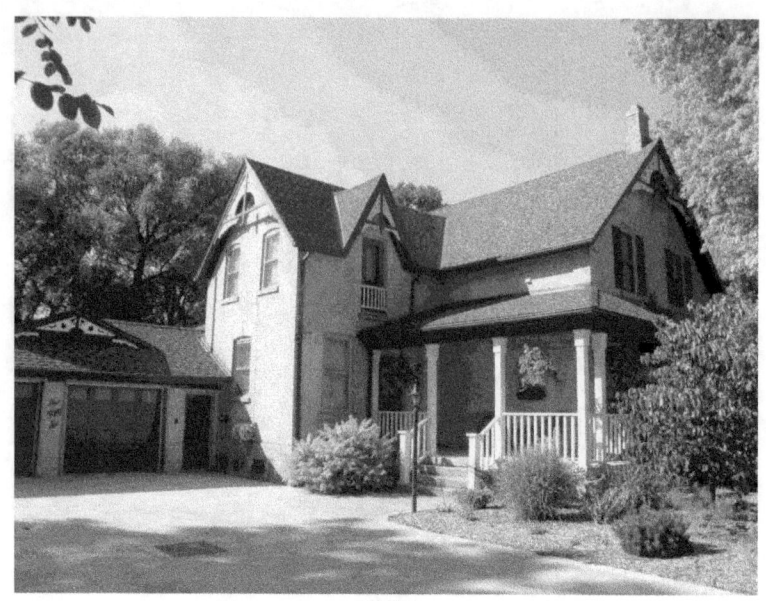

#156

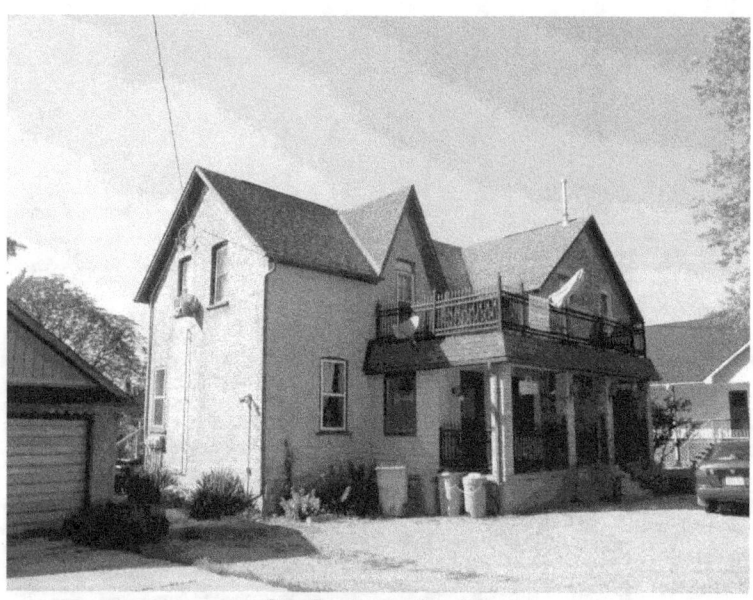

St. George Street

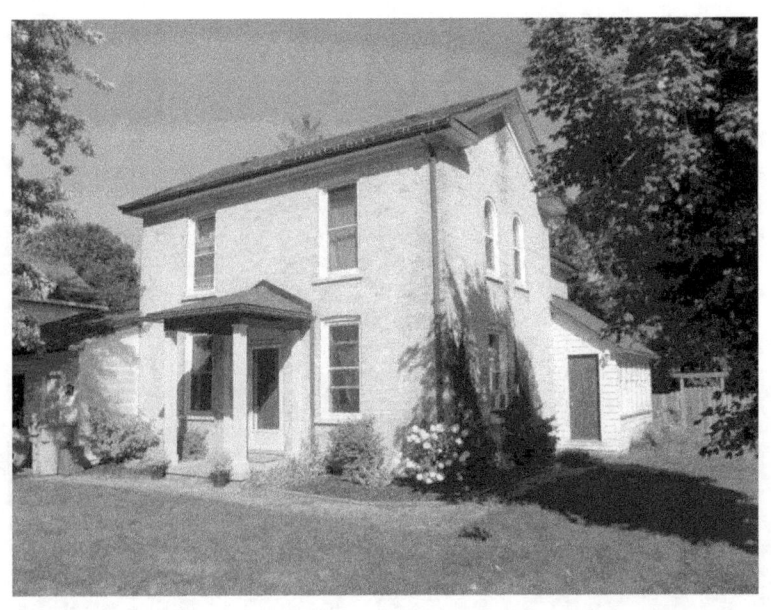

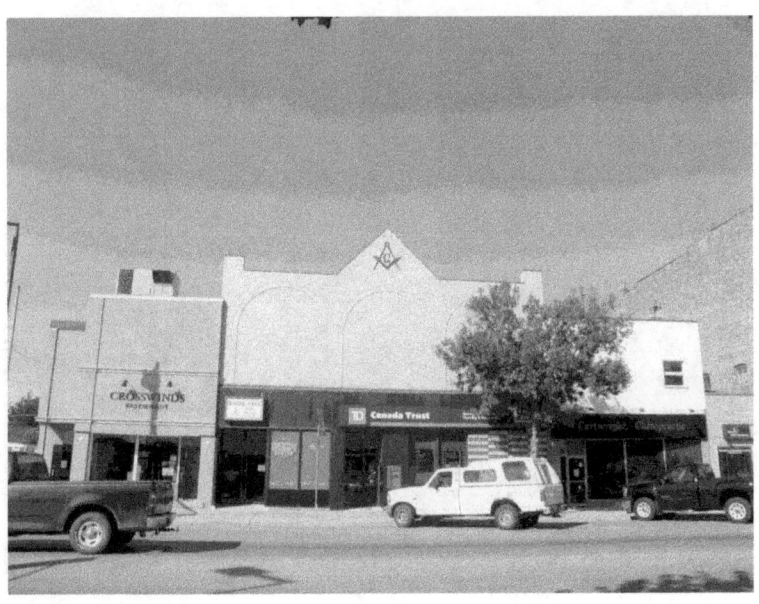

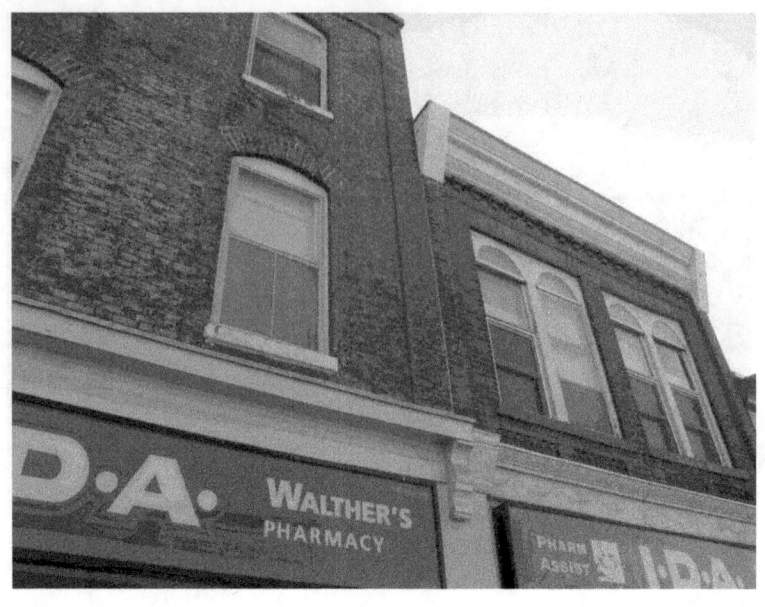

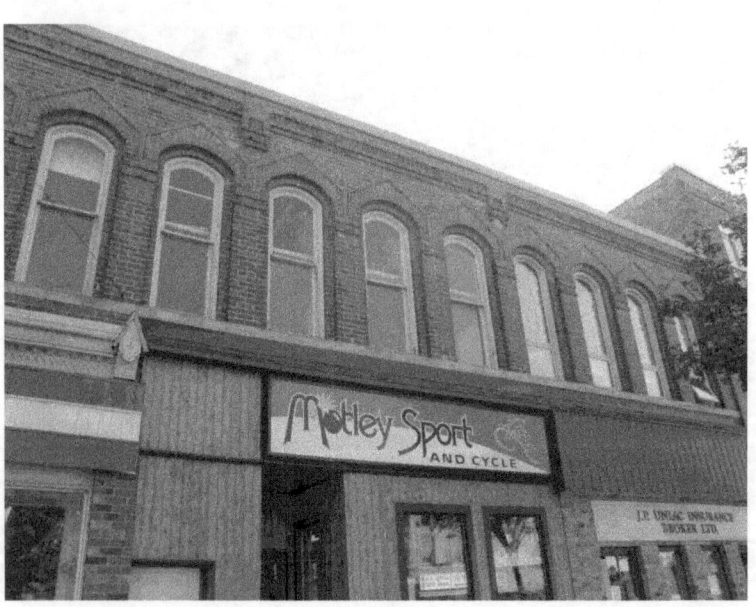

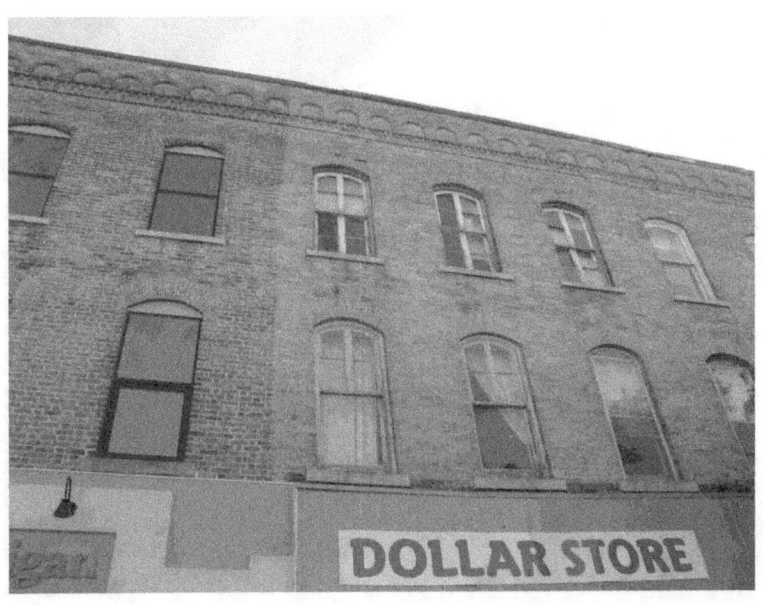

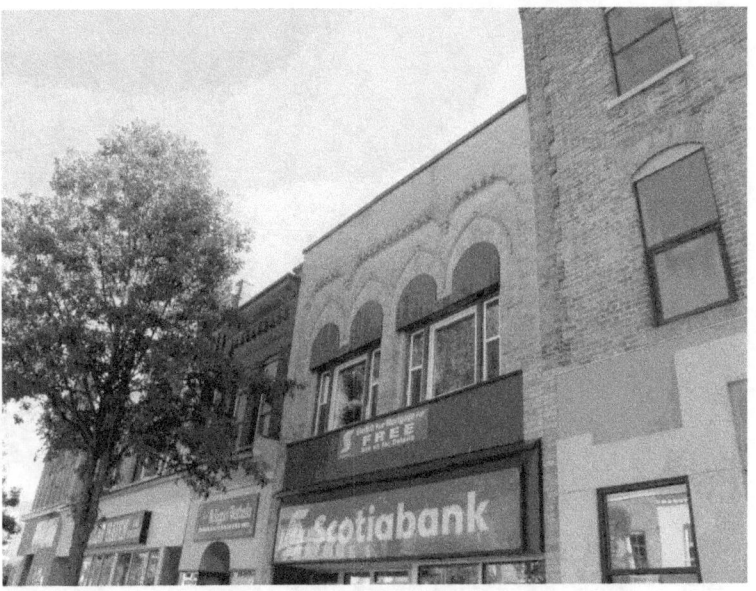

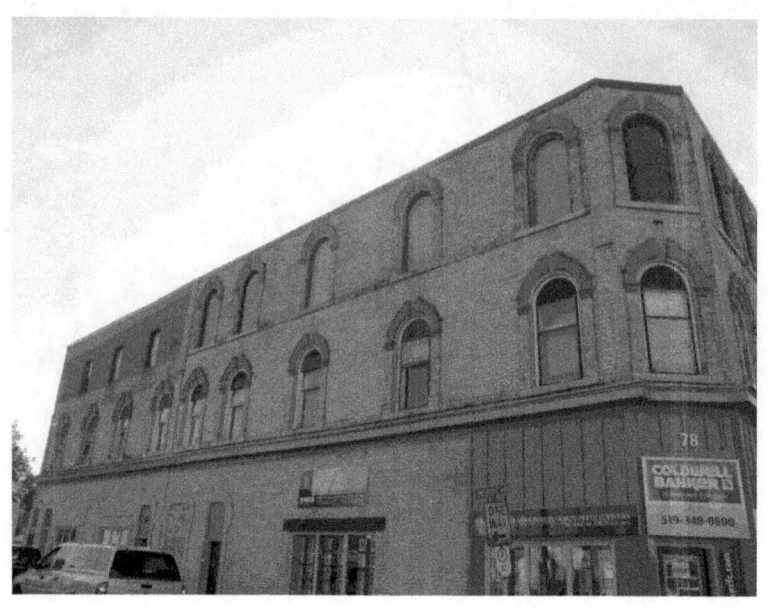

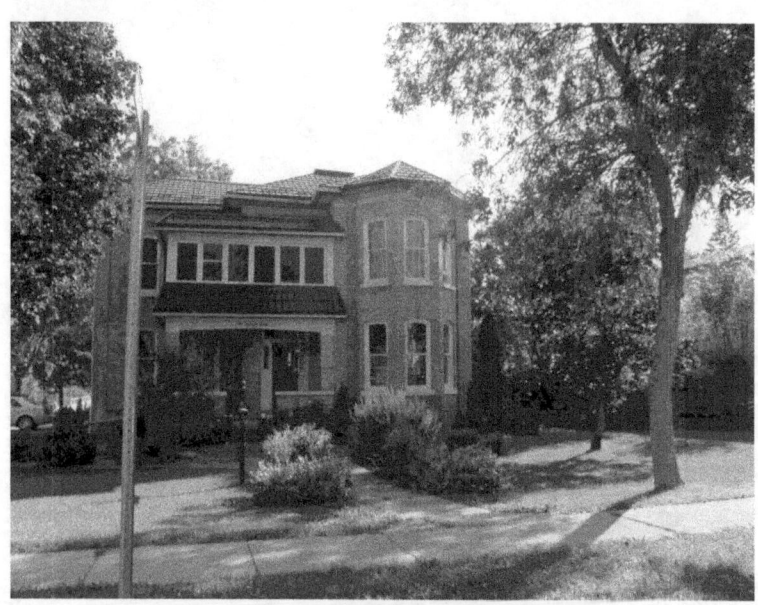

168 Ontario Road – yellow brick

Walton

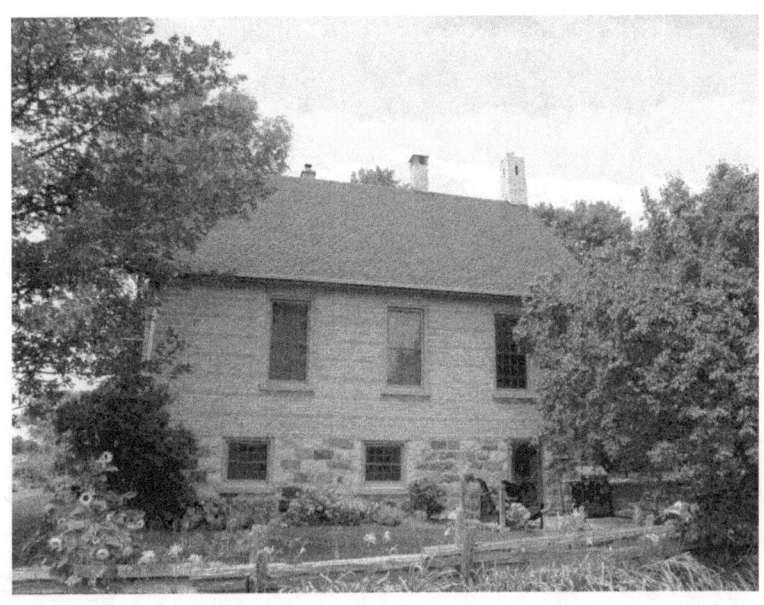

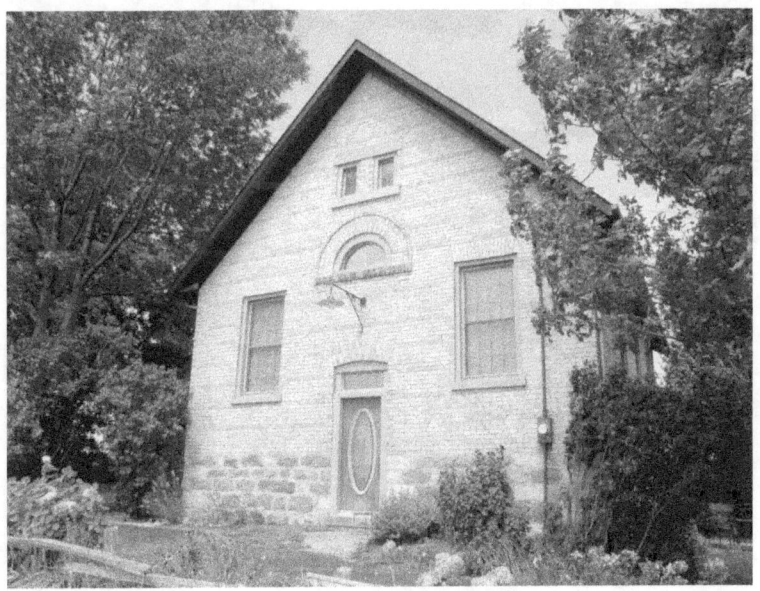

Whitechurch

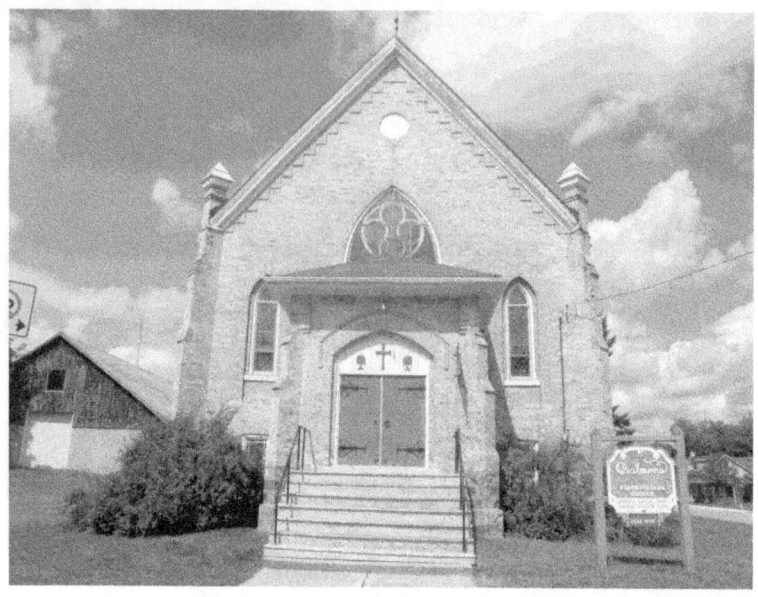

Chalmers Presbyterian Church

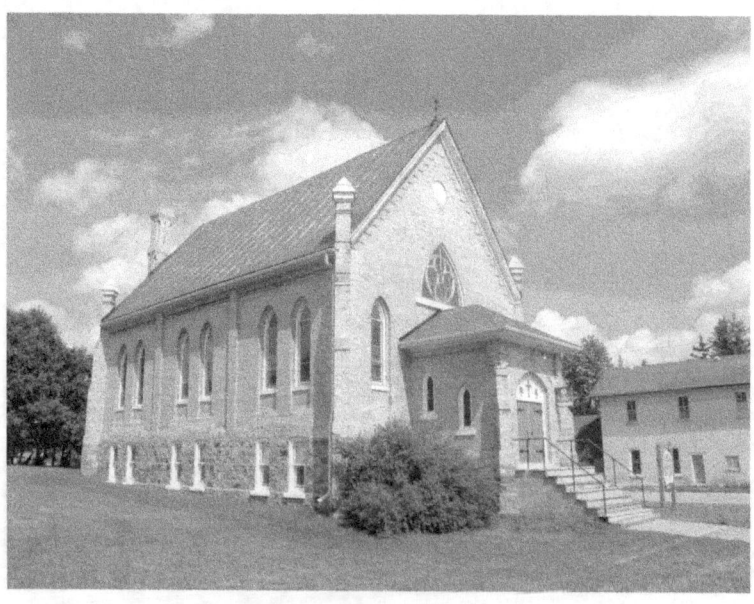

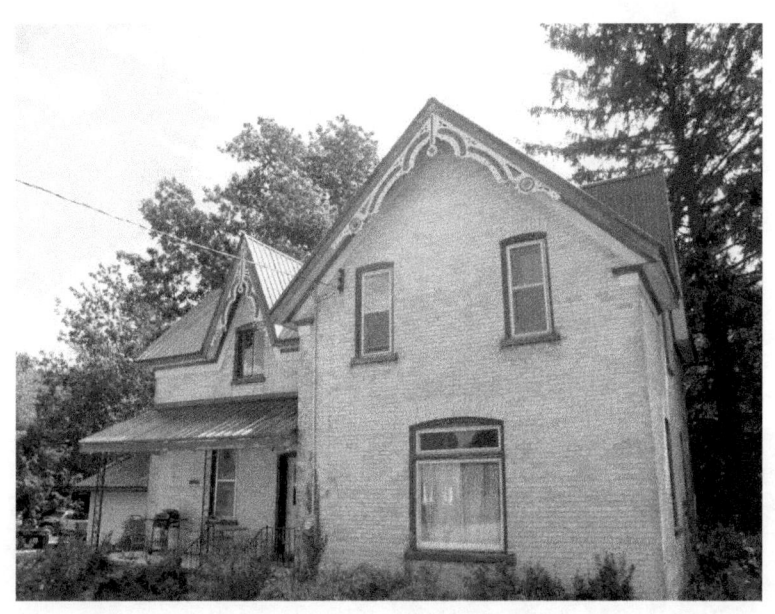

Winthrop

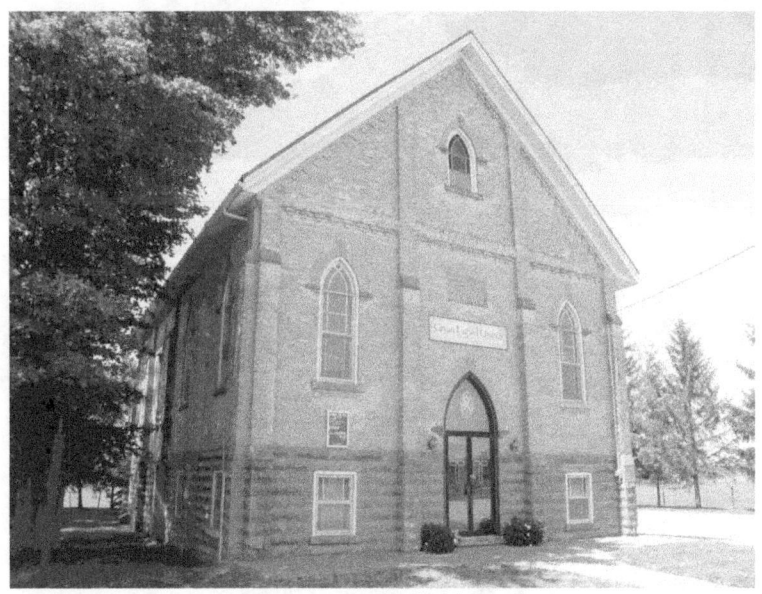

Cavan United Church

www.ingramcontent.com/pod-product-compliance
Lightning Source LLC
Chambersburg PA
CBHW071543170526
45166CB00004B/1530